CLARITY Media

CW01313139

Celebrating 20 years of puzzles 2005-2025

Published by Clarity Media Ltd www.clarity-media.co.uk

Content created by Izzy Newton, Patrick Creek, Dan Moore and Andy Harwood

Design and layout by Andy Harwood

About Clarity Media

Clarity Media are a leading provider of a huge range of puzzles for adults and children. Find out more at www.clarity-media.co.uk

Puzzle Magazines and Books

For downloadable PDF puzzle magazines, visit: www.puzzle-magazine.com

For a large range of puzzle books available to buy, visit: www.puzzle-book.co.uk

Puzzle Videos

To learn how to solve many different puzzles, why not visit the Clarity Media channel at: www.minURL.co.uk/youtube

Feedback and Ideas

We hope you really enjoy solving the puzzles in this book. If you have any comments on the book, ideas for new titles you'd like us to release or general feedback, please contact us via: www.clarity-media.co.uk/contactpuzzles.php

JANUARY 2025

Wednesday **1** — Lionel Messi

Lionel 'Leo' Messi is widely considered to be the greatest player of all time. He has won the Ballon d'Or a record seven times! He has also won 10 La Liga titles and five Champions Leagues with Barcelona, as well as two Ligue 1 titles with Paris Saint-Germain, and the World Cup and Copa América with Argentina!

Thursday **2** — Harry Kane

Before breaking into the Tottenham first team, Harry Kane went on several loan moves to lower-division clubs. Between 2011 and 2013 he played for Leyton Orient, Millwall, Norwich City and Leicester City.

Friday **3** — Harry Kane

He started playing regularly for Tottenham in 2014, and he made an immediate impact. He scored 31 goals in his first full season, and was named PFA Young Player of the Year.

Saturday **4** — Harry Kane

He went on to score 280 goals for Tottenham, overtaking Jimmy Greaves to become Spurs' all-time top-scorer. Despite these exploits, he never won a single trophy!

Sunday **5** — Harry Kane

Kane moved to Bayern Munich in 2023, and he finished his first season as Bundesliga top-scorer, scoring more than a goal a game! His wait for his first ever trophy continued, however, as Bayern failed to win the Bundesliga for the first time since 2011!

ENGLAND

Euro 24 final

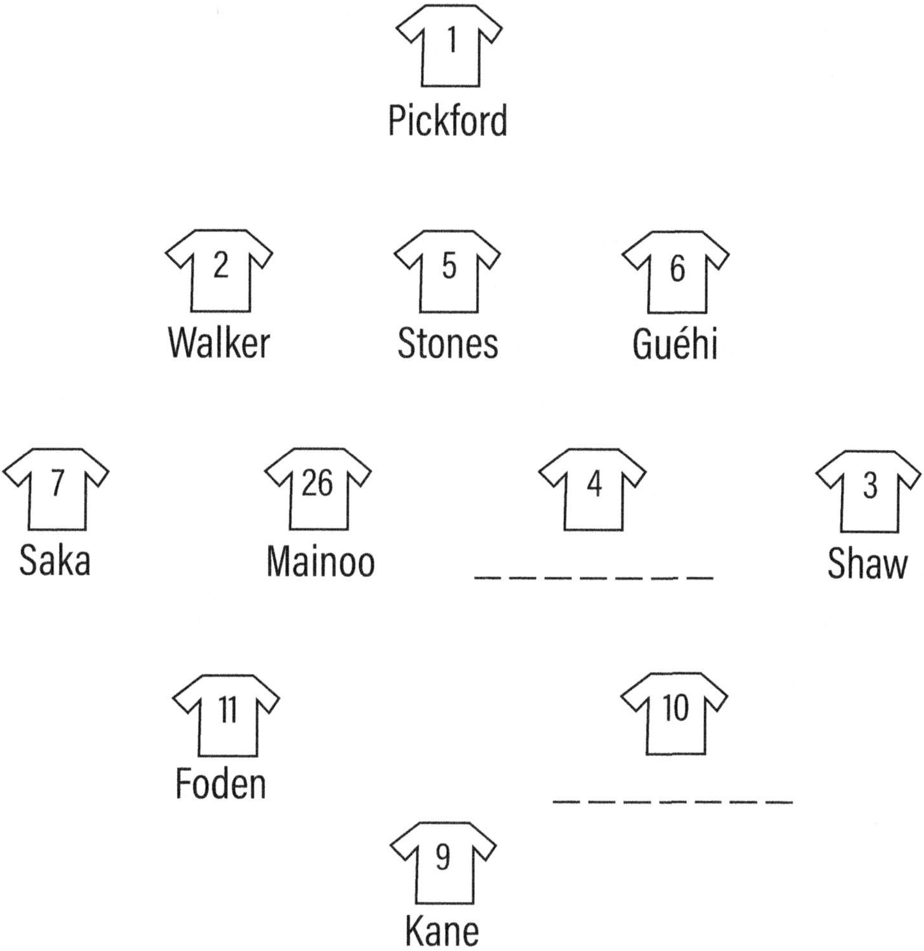

Manager: **Gareth Southgate**

This is England's starting lineup from the Euro 2024 final.
Can you fill in the two missing players?

Monday **6** Harry Kane

Kane is also England's all-time top scorer, with 62 goals in 89 appearances. He made his debut as a substitute against Lithuania in 2015, and he scored with his very first touch!

Tuesday **7** Jude Bellingham

21-year-old Jude Bellingham has already achieved remarkable things in his short career. He made his debut for Birmingham City in 2019 at the age of just 16, and he made such an impact that when he left the club the following season his shirt number was retired!

Wednesday **8** Jude Bellingham

He was sold to Borussia Dortmund in 2020 for £25 million, which made him the most expensive 17-year-old in history!

Thursday **9** Jude Bellingham

While playing for Dortmund he established himself as one of the best players in the Bundesliga. In 2023 he was named Bundesliga Player of the Season. He also won the prestigious Kopa trophy, which is awarded to the best young player in the world.

Friday **10** Jude Bellingham

His three years in Germany earned him a transfer to Real Madrid, for a reported €103 million. He made an immediate impact in Spain, scoring 10 goals in his first 10 games! (Cristiano Ronaldo achieved the same feat, when he moved to the club in 2009.) He is now considered by many to be the best player in the world!

Saturday **11** The Bellinghams

Jude's younger brother, Jobe, also played for Birmingham City before transferring to Sunderland. The Bellinghams' father, Mark Bellingham, was a professional footballer too – and a police sergeant.

Sunday **12** Kylian Mbappé

Kylian Mbappé made his debut for Monaco in 2015, at the age of 16 years and 347 days. This made him Monaco's youngest ever player, beating the previous record held by Thierry Henry.

Chelsea captain:

N O

Y H J

E T

R

R

Write your answer on the line below (4,5):

_ _ _ _   _ _ _ _ _

Monday **13** — Kylian Mbappé

The following season Mbappé's Monaco team, which also included Fabinho and Bernardo Silva, interrupted Paris Saint-Germain's period of dominance by winning the Ligue 1 title. They also reach the semi-final of the Champions League, but were knocked out by Juventus.

Tuesday **14** — Kylian Mbappé

Mbappé moved to PSG the following season for a reported fee of €180 million, making him the most expensive teenage player of all time.

Wednesday **15** — Kylian Mbappé

However, this was only the second-highest fee of all time, because PSG had just paid €222 million to buy Neymar from Barcelona!

Thursday **16** — Vinícius Júnior

Vini Jr moved from the Brazillian team Flamengo to Real Madrid in 2018, at the age of 17. He made his debut against Atlético Madrid in September 2018, becoming the first player born in the 21st Century to play for Real.

Friday **17** — Vinícius Júnior

His Real Madrid teammate Jude Bellingham described him as 'probably the best player in the world.'

Saturday **18** — Rodri

Rodri has often been compared to the great Barcelona midfielder Sergio Busquets, so it is perhaps surprising that he started his career at Barca's more defensive rivals Atlético Madrid.

Sunday **19** — Rodri

He moved to Manchester City in 2019 as a replacement for Fernandinho, and he quickly established himself as one of the best defensive-midfielders in the world.

PUZZLE 3 SPOT THE DIFFERENCE

Can you spot the six differences between the two images?

Monday **20** Erling Haaland

Erling Braut Haaland is the son of Alf-Inge Haaland, a Norwegian right back/ midfielder who played for Nottingham Forest, Leeds United and Manchester City in the 1990s and early 2000s. His mother, Gry Marita Braut, is a former heptathlon athlete.

Tuesday **21** Erling Haaland

The younger Haaland started his career in Norway at Bryne and Molde, before moving to Red Bull Salzburg. He scored a remarkable 17 goals in 16 appearances for Salzburg, which quickly earned him a move to Borussia Dortmund.

Wednesday **22** Erling Haaland

Haaland's goalscoring statistics are remarkable. He scored 62 goals in 67 appearances for Dortmund, and in his first season at Manchester City he scored 36 goals in 35 appearances (that's more than a goal a game)!

Thursday **23** Erling Haaland

His Champions League record is especially impressive – so far he has scored 41 goals in just 37 appearances!

Friday **24** Erling Haaland

At the age of 23, he has already scored more Champions League goals than the likes of Sergio Agüero, Gerd Müller, Samuel Eto'o and Wayne Rooney!

Saturday **25** Bukayo Saka

At the age of just 22, Arsenal and England winger Bukayo Saka has already reached 200 games for his club, and has played in a World Cup and two European Championships!

Sunday **26** Bukayo Saka

His teammates call him 'Little Chilli,' which is a nickname given to him by former Arsenal striker Pierre-Emerick Aubameyang.

PUZZLE 4 ANAGRAM CHALLENGE

Premier League manager:

I N A

G

E R

H

T

E K

Write your answer on the line below (4,3,3):

_ _ _ _   _ _ _   _ _ _

Monday **27** — England's Top Goalscorer

Wayne Rooney was England's top goalscorer from 2015 to 2023, when Kane took over. Before Rooney, Bobby Charlton held the record for over 40 years.

Tuesday **28** — Mohamed Salah

After playing in his native Egypt for Al Mokawloon Al Arab, Mohamed Salah made his breakthrough at the Swiss club Basel. He was awarded the Swiss Super League Player of the Year for his first season in 2013.

Wednesday **29** — Mohamed Salah

This earned him a move to Chelsea, but he made little impact for the Blues. He played just 13 times in two years, and scored two goals. (He has this in common with Kevin de Bruyne, who signed for Chelsea in 2012 and made just three appearances.)

Thursday **30** — Mohamed Salah

After a successful stint in Italy with Fiorentina and Roma, he moved to Liverpool in 2017, and the rest is history. He was instrumental in Liverpool's Premier League and Champions League winning teams, and he has won the Premier League Golden Boot three times!

Friday **31** — Mohamed Salah

In the 2018 Egyptian presidential elections, Salah received more than a million votes – despite not standing as a candidate!

Saturday **1** — Bernardo Silva

Since signing from Monaco in 2017, Bernardo has become one of Manchester City's most important players. City manager Pep Guardiola has described him as 'one of the best players I have ever seen.'

Sunday **2** — Bernardo Silva

While he is most often deployed as either a central midfielder or a right winger, Bernardo has played in many different positions for Man City, including attacking midfielder, second striker, deep-lying playmaker, wing back, and even centre forward (albeit in a creative 'false 9' role).

UEFA Champions League Winners

A	S	R	E	P	U	A	E	S	L	E	H	C	M	K
C	R	B	O	S	Z	E	J	C	L	B	E	A	I	F
I	E	H	M	V	S	L	O	U	R	P	R	A	I	U
F	A	A	C	E	S	L	O	O	V	S	X	N	A	O
N	L	E	A	I	T	R	B	O	E	E	T	A	R	Z
E	L	T	P	N	N	M	E	I	P	E	N	E	J	F
B	I	L	I	D	Q	U	L	G	R	R	A	T	E	A
S	V	C	V	H	S	L	M	M	R	L	E	Y	U	S
A	N	E	P	O	E	E	I	N	M	U	E	V	U	S
L	O	L	N	V	I	L	D	A	R	N	B	R	I	O
K	T	T	O	E	A	U	D	S	O	E	N	M	T	L
L	S	I	T	N	D	R	M	O	X	V	Y	E	A	J
J	A	C	R	Q	I	S	R	U	R	Q	D	A	B	H
S	P	U	O	D	F	D	E	C	Y	P	R	Q	B	O
R	O	E	P	O	L	B	A	R	C	E	L	O	N	A

AJAX
ASTON VILLA
BARCELONA
BAYERN MUNICH
BENFICA
CELTIC
CHELSEA
FEYENOORD
HAMBURGER SV
INTER MILAN
JUVENTUS
LIVERPOOL
MARSEILLE
PORTO
PSV EINDHOVEN
REAL MADRID

Find each of the words in the grid of letters. Words may be hidden horizontally, vertically or diagonally and in either a forwards or backwards direction.

FEBRUARY 2025 WEEK 5

Monday **3** Victor Osimhen

Victor Osimhen first came to prominence during the 2015 Under-17 World Cup in Chile. He was the breakout star of the Nigeria team who won the tournament, scoring 10 goals in seven games!

Tuesday **4** Victor Osimhen

Five years later, he realised his early potential in France – he was the star player of the Lille team which beat PSG to the Ligue 1 title in 2020-21!

Wednesday **5** Victor Osimhen

This earned him a €70 million move to Napoli (making him the most expensive African player of all time). In his second season in Italy, he won the Serie A title and finished top-scorer with 26 goals.

Thursday **6** Khvicha Kvaratskhelia

Georgian winger Khvicha Kvaratskhelia was named Serie A MVP and Champions League young player of the season in his first year at Napoli in 2022/23. This earned him the nickname Kvaradona (after Napoli's greatest-ever player, Diego Maradona).

Friday **7** Phil Foden

Phil Foden is a Manchester City die-hard, having been a fan since childhood. He joined the club's academy at the age of four and has progressed through the ranks to become a key player for both club and country.

Saturday **8** Phil Foden

He won the Under-17 World Cup in 2017, and he was awarded the Golden Ball.

Sunday **9** Phil Foden

He has been named both Premier League Young Player of the Season and PFA Young Player of the Year, and he is the youngest player ever to receive a Premier League winner's medal (in 2018).

roatian footballer:

L R

D

O

K

I U A

M Ć

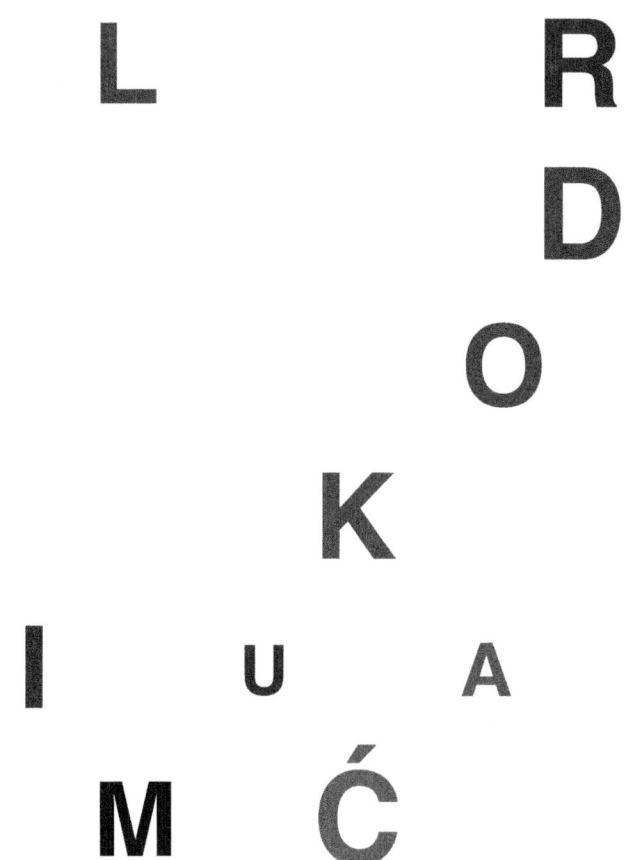

Write your answer on the line below (4,6):

_ _ _ _ _ _ _ _ _ _

Monday **10** — Antoine Griezmann

After five impressive seasons at Atlético Madrid Antoine Griezmann signed for Barcelona in 2019 for a fee of €120 million!

Tuesday **11** — Antoine Griezmann

His time at Barca was viewed as a disappointment, but since moving back to Atlético in 2021, he has reestablished himself as one of the best players in the world.

Wednesday **12** — Ilkay Gündogan

Before moving to Pep Guardiola's Manchester City in 2016, Gündogan played for Borussia Dortmund under manager Jürgen Klopp, making him one of just five players who have played for both managers (the others are Mario Götze, Xherdan Shaqiri, Thiago Alcântara, and Robert Lewandowski).

Thursday **13** — Robert Lewandowski

Polish striker Rober Lewandowski is one of the world's great goalscorers. He has scored over 500 goals in his career!

Friday **14** — Robert Lewandowski

In one 2015 match between Bayern Munich and Wolfsburg, he scored five goals in nine minutes!

Saturday **15** — Declan Rice

English defensive-midfielder Declan Rice moved from West Ham United to Arsenal in 2023 for a fee of £105 million, making him the most expensive British player of all time!

Sunday **16** — Declan Rice

He has become one of England's most important players, but he represented the Republic of Ireland at youth level.

Can you identify which football is at the bottom of the stack?

Monday **17** — Kevin De Bruyne

De Bruyne signed for Chelsea in 2012 from the Belgian team Genk, but he made only three appearances for the club.

Tuesday **18** — Kevin De Bruyne

He was sold to VfL Wolfsburg in 2014, and the following year he was named Germany's Footballer of the Year, after scoring 16 goals and providing 27 assists!

Wednesday **19** — Kevin De Bruyne

He moved to Manchester City in 2015 for a club-record fee of £55 million. He is now the star player for the best team in the Premier League – Chelsea must be kicking themselves!

Thursday **20** — Kevin De Bruyne

De Bruyne is right-footed, but he is skilled with his left foot as well. This is because when he played in his garden as a child, his parents told him to shoot with his left foot, because his powerful right-footed strikes kept breaking their flower pots!

Friday **21** — Lautaro Martínez

Inter Milan's Argentine striker Lautaro Martínez is known for his impressive collection of tattoos. His first tattoo was a tribute to his grandfather, which he got when he was just 14!

Saturday **22** — Ederson

In addition to his shot-stopping abilities, Ederson is known for his exceptional passing and control on the ball. Former Man City goalkeeper Shay Given called him 'the best goalkeeper in the world with his feet'.

Sunday **23** — John Stones

Manchester City's English centre-back John Stones is one of the most technically skilful defenders in the world, and he is capable of playing in both midfield and defense.

Football Club Nicknames

S	L	K	F	J	I	J	E	G	U	N	N	E	R	S
E	E	H	U	T	B	O	R	O	W	S	R	R	O	A
U	V	I	R	B	M	E	Q	H	N	V	O	T	J	H
L	R	R	R	L	V	R	R	P	S	M	Y	U	L	O
B	S	R	R	A	G	H	H	H	A	B	A	Z	S	O
T	R	E	S	D	N	Y	O	G	V	T	L	E	H	P
S	E	D	R	E	E	A	P	I	H	A	S	T	P	S
A	G	D	E	S	H	I	C	L	P	M	W	O	P	L
E	A	E	T	E	E	R	T	W	O	A	E	Z	O	F
M	T	V	T	S	B	L	A	C	K	C	A	T	S	O
P	T	I	A	T	H	A	S	J	N	P	I	J	E	X
C	O	L	H	B	S	R	L	I	T	A	C	U	L	E
Z	C	S	C	Q	E	R	O	B	I	N	S	I	Y	S
U	P	Y	V	T	W	H	I	T	E	S	Z	W	U	A
L	U	D	I	A	L	L	I	V	Q	I	I	A	C	T

BLACK CATS
BLADES
BLUES
BORO
CANARIES
COTTAGERS
FOXES
GUNNERS
HATTERS
HOOPS
MAGPIES
RED DEVILS
ROBINS
ROYALS
VILLA
WHITES

Find each of the words in the grid of letters. Words may be hidden horizontally, vertically or diagonally and in either a forwards or backwards direction.

Monday **24** — Martin Ødegaard

Martin Ødegaard was a teenage prodigy who started playing professionally for the Norwegian team Strømsgodset in 2014 at the age of just 15! He made his debut for the Norwegian national team the same year!

Tuesday **25** — Martin Ødegaard

In 2015, at the age of 16, he became the youngest player ever to sign for Real Madrid! He was on their books for five years, but he struggled to break into the first team. He made just eight appearances, and was loaned out to the Dutch teams Heerenveen and Vitesse, and to the Spanish team Real Sociedad.

Wednesday **26** — Martin Ødegaard

He began to fulfil his potential when he moved to Arsenal in 2021. He is one of the key players in Mikel Arteta's team, and he was named club captain at the age of just 23!

Thursday **27** — Julián Álvarez

Before moving to Manchester City in 2022, Julián Álvarez played in Argentina for River Plate. In one Copa Libertadores match against the Peruvian champions Alianza Lima, Álvarez scored six goals for River!

Friday **28** — Jamal Musiala

Jamal Musiala is one of the stars of the German national team, but he could have played for England. He was born in Stuttgart, but he grew up in London, and he represented England at youth level.

Saturday **1** — Jamal Musiala

His Bayern Munich teammate Leroy Sané gave him the nickname 'Bambi' because he's 'quite a pleasant guy.'

Sunday **2** — Rúben Dias

Manchester City's Portuguese centre-back Rúben Dias was named Premier League Player of the Season for 2020–21, making him one of just four defenders who have won the award. (The others are Nemanja Vidić, Virgil van Dijk, and Dias's Man City predecessor Vincent Kompany.)

PUZZLE 9 DREAM TEAM

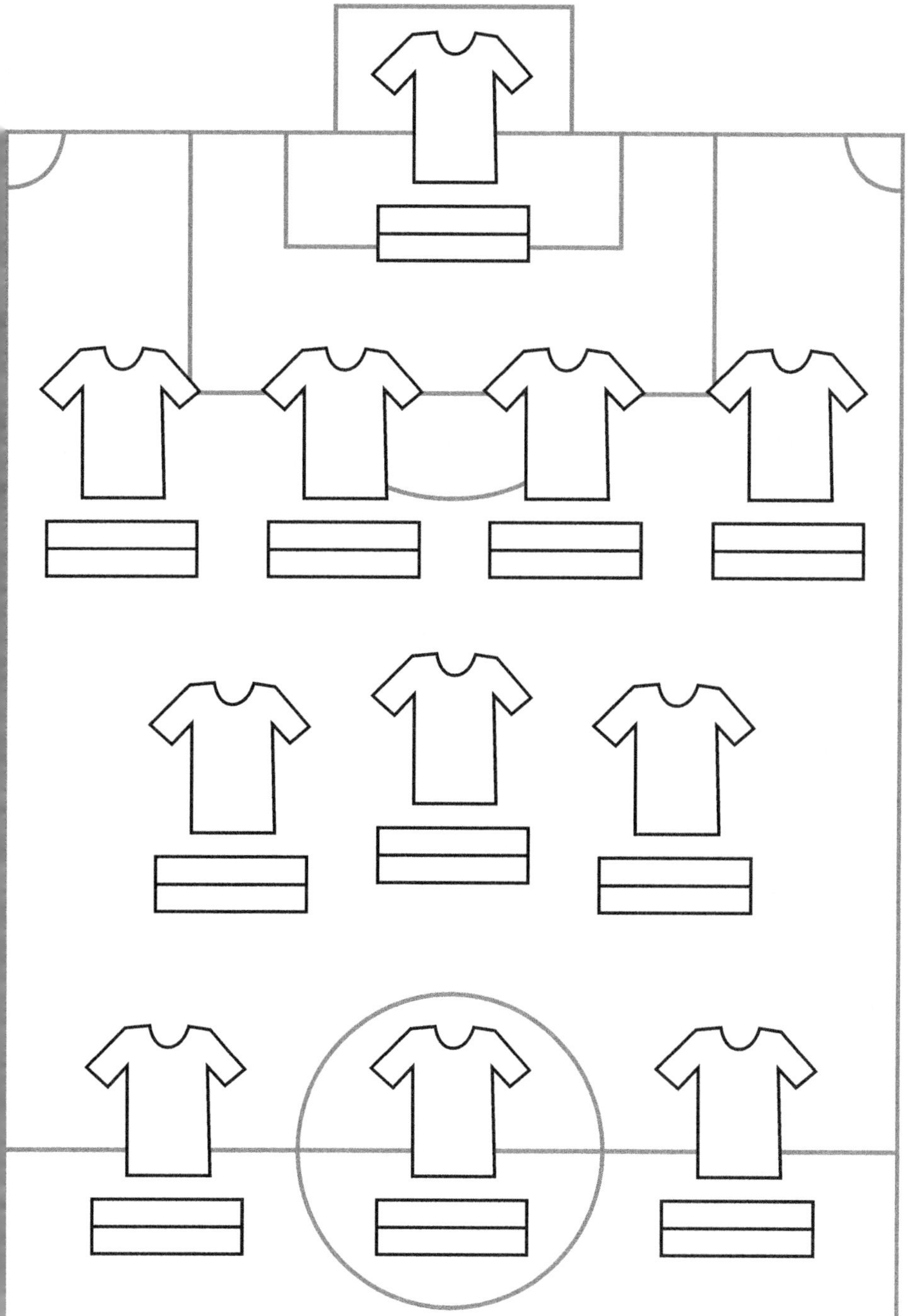

Use this space to design your perfect team! Pick your favourite goalkeeper, your four favourite defenders, your three favourite midfielders, and your three favourite forwards.

Monday **3** — Son Heung-min

Tottenham forward Son Heung-min is a superstar in his native South Korea, and is widely regarded as the greatest Asian footballer of all time.

Tuesday **4** — Son Heung-min

In 2022 he became the first Asian player ever to win the Premier League Golden Boot (he scored 23 goals).

Wednesday **5** — Son Heung-min

In 2020, Son scored a remarkable goal against Burnley, which was awarded the coveted Puskás Award, given to the scorer of the 'most beautiful' goal of the calendar year.

Thursday **6** — Luka Modrić

Croatian midfielder Luka Modrić won the Ballon d'Or in 2018, making him the only player other than Cristiano Ronaldo or Lionel Messi to win the award between 2008 and 2021!

Friday **7** — Nicolò Barella

Inter Milan midfielder Nicolò Barella is widely regarded as one of the best players in Serie A. He has been compared to both Steven Gerrard and N'Golo Kanté.

Saturday **8** — Gavi

At the age of just 19, Spanish midfielder Gavi has established himself as one of Barcelona's most important players. He has been compared to Barca greats Xavi and Andrés Iniesta.

Sunday **9** — Rafael Leão

AC Milan winger Rafael Leão is known as the 'Portuguese Mbappé.' He has also been compared to Cristiano Ronaldo.

Midfielder:

N E

I L

C

R

D C

E A

Write your answer on the line below (6,4):

_ _ _ _ _ _   _ _ _ _

Monday **10** — Federico Valverde

As a young player, Real Madrid's Uruguayan midfielder Federico Valverde's nickname was Pajarito, which means 'baby bird.' He is now known as Halcón, which means 'falcon.'

Tuesday **11** — Marc-André ter Stegen

Like his German compatriot Manuel Neuer, Barcelona goalkeeper Marc-André ter Stegen is often refferred to as a 'sweeper keeper,' because of his exceptional abilities on the ball.

Wednesday **12** — Karim Benzema

Between 2014 and 2018, French striker Karim Benzema was part of Real Madrid's famous 'BBC' front three, alongside Cristiano Ronaldo and Gareth Bale.

Thursday **13** — Karim Benzema

Benzema tended to fly under the radar in those years, but after the departure of Bale and Ronaldo, he became Real's star player, winning the Ballon d'Or in 2022.

Friday **14** — Thibaut Courtois

Belgian goalkeeper Thibaut Courtois took Petr Čech's place in the Chelsea first team in 2015, even though Čech had won the Premier League Golden Glove award for the previous season!

Saturday **15** — Pedri

Spanish midfielder Pedri made his debut for Barcelona at the age of 18, and played 73 times in his first full season!

Sunday **16** — Rodrygo

At the age of 11, Real Madrid forward Rodrygo became the youngest athlete to sign a sponsorship deal with Nike. The following year he was dubbed 'the new Neymar' by the Brazillian media.

Defenders

P	S	A	K	O	Q	E	H	E	O	R	R	E	I	H
N	E	E	K	F	B	G	A	K	A	I	H	O	S	J
E	P	P	R	I	D	L	N	V	R	V	A	Y	J	O
S	K	W	E	G	N	E	C	E	I	B	D	V	V	F
L	A	N	F	U	I	H	T	S	A	J	A	I	C	Y
O	H	U	E	E	H	N	Z	H	D	F	R	S	M	I
O	S	S	Q	R	S	G	H	Y	L	R	T	N	N	O
B	X	C	F	O	Y	Z	E	O	A	M	I	I	R	W
P	J	I	V	A	L	R	U	N	M	V	D	X	A	B
U	L	R	Q	S	V	F	E	F	V	L	Z	U	I	R
Y	U	E	H	N	I	B	K	H	A	H	O	F	G	P
O	I	A	E	H	N	C	X	M	Z	D	I	A	V	I
L	Z	Q	C	X	H	K	A	R	C	X	S	C	F	Q
W	C	U	I	W	O	C	A	L	O	R	A	P	G	U
Q	B	A	R	E	S	I	N	E	V	H	P	C	H	E

ALDAIR
BARESI
BENARRIVO
CAFU
FIGUEROA
HIERRO
LUIZ
MALDINI
OLSEN
PAROLA
PEPE
PIQUE
PUYOL
SCIREA
SERGINHO
SYLVINHO

Find each of the words in the grid of letters. Words may be hidden horizontally, vertically or diagonally and in either a forwards or backwards direction.

Monday **17** — Kim Min-jae

27-year-old South Korean centre-back Kim Min-jae has spent most of his career in Asia, playing for teams like Jeonbuk Hyundai Motors and Beijing Guoan. He moved to Napoli in 2022, and was a key part of the team which won the 2022-23 Serie A title. He is now one of the most highly-rated defenders in the world!

Tuesday **18** — William Saliba

Arsenal centre-back William Saliba started out as a striker, and he was coached by Kylian Mbappé's father as a child!

Wednesday **19** — Kyle Walker

Manchester City right-back Kyle Walker is one of the fastest players in the Premier League, reaching top speeds of 37.31km/h!

Thursday **20** — Micky van de Ven

Tottenham's Micky van de Ven is even quicker. He became the Premier League's fastest player of all time in January 2024 when he ran at over 38 km/h in a game against Brentford!

Friday **21** — Emiliano Martínez

Aston Villa goalkeeper Emiliano Martínez won the Lev Yashin award for best goalkeeper at the 2023 Ballon d'Or ceremony, after winning the World Cup with Argentina.

Saturday **22** — Florian Wirtz

German winger Florian Wirtz was instrumental in Bayer Leverkusen's Bundesliga title-winning team in 2024.

Sunday **23** — Jack Grealish

Jack Grealish started his career at Aston Villa, which is the team his great-great-grandfather, Billy Garraty played for. Garraty won the FA Cup with Villa in 1905!

panish footballer:

O

R D

R

I

Write your answer on the line below (5):

_ _ _ _ _

Monday **24** — Achraf Hakimi

PSG right-back Achraf Hakimi was one of the stars of the Morocco team which reached the semi-final of the 2022 World Cup.

Tuesday **25** — Bayer Leverkusen

Bayer 04 Leverkusen are so called because they were founded in 1904 by the employees of Bayer AG, which is a German pharmaceutical company based in Leverkusen.

Wednesday **26** — Bayer Leverkusen

They were first promoted to the Bundesliga (the top division of German football) in 1979, and have remained there ever since.

Thursday **27** — Bayer Leverkusen

In their history they have won one UEFA Cup, one DFB-Pokal (Germany's equivalent of the FA Cup), and they were runners-up in the 2001/02 Champions League (they lost to Real Madrid).

Friday **28** — Bayer Leverkusen

They also finished second in the Bundesliga a record five times between 1997 and 2011, without ever winning the title. This earned them the nickname 'Bayer Neverkusen.'

Saturday **29** — Olivier Giroud

Former Arsenal and Chelsea striker Olivier Giroud is France's all-time top scorer, ahead of the likes of Thierry Henry, Kylian Mbappé, Michel Platini and Karim Benzema.

Sunday **30** — Olivier Giroud

At the age of 38, he is still playing professionally for Los Angeles FC.

England Managers

R	N	S	U	R	O	T	U	H	F	N	A	Y	W	C
M	X	S	T	I	Y	R	D	E	O	T	R	E	E	N
N	A	G	E	E	K	G	T	S	R	M	D	I	L	O
M	L	B	L	P	T	A	S	R	O	C	T	V	D	S
O	R	K	P	A	G	K	U	Y	S	C	K	E	D	B
I	E	O	Y	H	I	F	E	O	T	L	U	R	O	O
D	U	L	T	R	R	S	H	S	O	A	R	P	H	R
Y	O	U	E	Z	M	E	C	Y	D	R	A	L	L	A
R	O	Y	E	A	T	U	G	F	E	E	E	T	W	V
S	F	I	R	W	I	I	H	N	R	N	D	A	T	L
U	N	O	S	G	D	O	H	R	E	C	R	A	E	P
G	R	E	E	N	W	O	O	D	V	V	O	B	Q	A
O	R	Z	C	A	P	E	L	L	O	U	R	P	S	X
P	M	O	T	T	O	B	R	E	T	N	I	W	C	S
W	K	P	T	V	E	N	A	B	L	E	S	L	S	L

ALLARDYCE
CAPELLO
ERIKSSON
GREENWOOD
HODDLE
HODGSON
KEEGAN
MCCLAREN
PEARCE
RAMSEY
REVIE
ROBSON
SOUTHGATE
TAYLOR
VENABLES
WINTERBOTTOM

Find each of the words in the grid of letters. Words may be hidden horizontally, vertically or diagonally and in either a forwards or backwards direction.

Monday **31** — Bayer Leverkusen

Leverkusen's fortunes changed in 2024 when manager Xabi Alonso led them to their first ever Bundesliga title!

Tuesday **1** — Bayer Leverkusen

Alonso took over in 2022 when the team were second-bottom in the Bundesliga, after eight games. In his first season they finished sixth and reached the final of the Europa League. The following season they went unbeaten for 33 games (a German record) and beat Bayern Munich to the Bundesliga title!

Wednesday **2** — Bayer Leverkusen

They lost the 2024 Europa League final to Atalanta – remarkably, this was the only game they lost in the entire 2023-24 season!

Thursday **3** — Bayer Leverkusen

They have had many great players over the years, including Ulf Kirsten, Michael Ballack and Jens Nowotny. Their current stars include Victor Boniface, Florian Wirtz and Granit Xhaka.

Friday **4** — Bruno Fernandes

Today, Portuguese midfielder Bruno Fernandes is one of Manchester United's most important players, but as a teenager he had a poster of former Manchester City defender Stephen Ireland on his wall!

Saturday **5** — Chelsea

Today Chelsea are one of the world's richest and most successful teams, but in the 1980s their finances were in such a bad state that businessman Ken Bates bought the club for £1!

Sunday **6** — Chelsea

Their fortunes turned around in the late 90s, when they brought in exciting foreign players like Gianfranco Zola, Gianluca Vialli and Marcel Desailly. In 2003, Bates sold the club he had bought for £1 to Russian oligarch Roman Abramovich for £60 million!

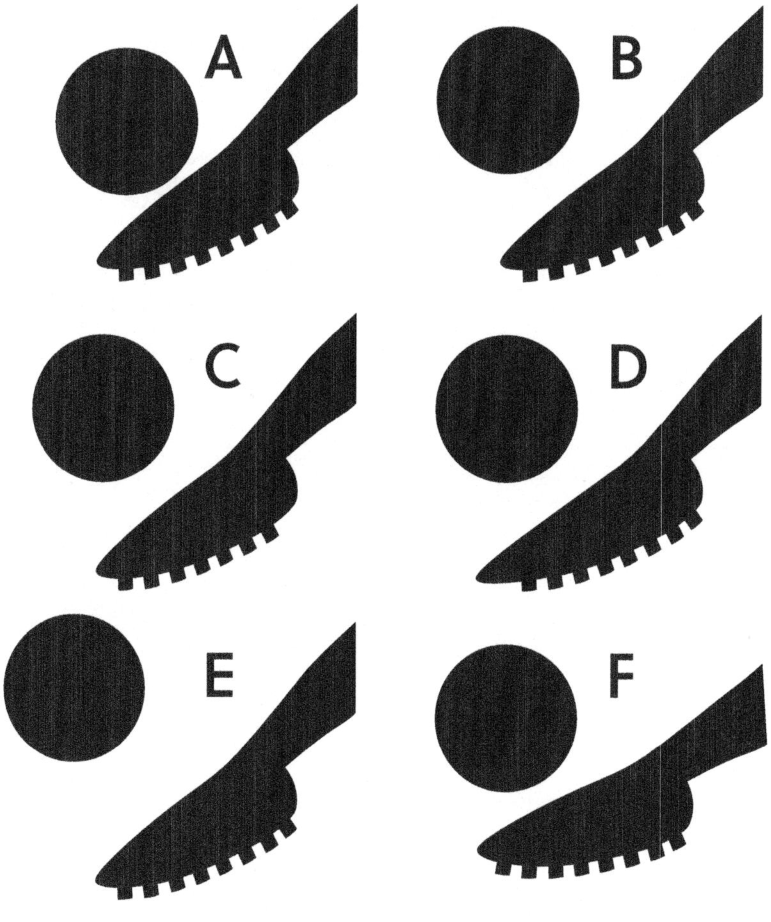

Can you identify which foot perfectly matches the top silhouette?

Monday **7** — Joshua Kimmich

German midfielder and right-back Joshua Kimmich made his debut for Bayern Munich in 2015, and he went on to win the Bundesliga with Bayern eight times in a row. 2023-24 was the first season in his professional career in which he did not win the Bundesliga!

Tuesday **8** — Dominik Szoboszlai

Liverpool midfielder Dominik Szoboszlai is a hero in his native Hungary. He was named captain of the Hungarian national team at the age of just 22, after his last-minute goal against Iceland sealed their place in Euro 2020.

Wednesday **9** — Trent Alexander-Arnold

Liverpool right-back Trent Alexander-Arnold holds the record for the most assists by a defender in the Premier League!

Thursday **10** — Alexis Mac Allister

Versatile midfielder Alexis Mac Allister moved from Brighton to Liverpool in 2023, after winning the 2022 World Cup with Argentina.

Friday **11** — Alexis Mac Allister

His nickname in the Liverpool dressing room is 'Gary,' after the Scottish midfielder Gary McAllister, who played for Liverpool in the early 2000s.

Saturday **12** — Arsenal

Arsenal was originally founded in 1886 by 16 munitions workers at the Royal Arsenal in Woolwich.

Sunday **13** — Arsenal

They were originally called Dial Square, which was the name of a workshop in the Royal Arsenal complex, but they were renamed Royal Arsenal within the first year.

razilian goalkeeper:

O

N

S R

D

E E

Write your answer on the line below (7):

_ _ _ _ _ _ _

Monday **14** Arsenal

In 1913, activists demanding the vote for women burned down part of the Manor Ground stadium, where Royal Arsenal played their games. As a result, in 1914 Arsenal moved north of the river to Highbury, and they remained there until 2006, when they moved to the Emirates Stadium in Holloway.

Tuesday **15** Bruno Guimarães

Brazilian midfielder Bruno Guimarães made an immediate impact when he signed for Newcastle from Lyon in 2022. He scored with an impressive back-heel volley in his very first game!

Wednesday **16** Federico Dimarco

Italian wing-back Federico Dimarco is a key part of Simone Inzaghi's Serie A title-winning Inter Milan team, and is considered by many to be one of the best left-backs in the world.

Thursday **17** André Onana

Cameroonian goalkeeper André Onana has had a rocky time at Manchester United, but he was a key part of both the Ajax team which reached the semi-final of the Champions League in 2019, and the Inter Milan team which reached the final in 2023!

Friday **18** Victor Boniface

In 2023, Nigerian striker Victor Boniface reached the quarter-final of the Europa League with Belgian team Union Saint-Gilloise. He also finished joint top-scorer with Marcus Rashford. The following season, he moved to Bayer Leverkusen and won the Bundesliga!

Saturday **19** AC Milan

AC Milan was founded in 1899 as 'Milan Foot-ball and Cricket Club' by Englishman Herbert Kilpin.

Sunday **20** AC Milan

This is why – even in Italy – the club is named Milan, which is the city's English name, rather than the Italian Milano.

European Golden Shoe Winners

M	I	M	P	V	O	K	E	H	Z	S	N	F	Z	U
A	T	N	B	O	V	E	N	K	Q	D	H	V	T	L
K	S	A	L	K	N	A	R	K	W	P	L	R	N	E
A	H	L	Y	B	I	M	Z	B	M	O	U	D	C	W
A	S	R	L	L	I	N	O	T	H	L	C	R	G	A
Y	U	O	S	W	O	E	E	I	K	S	W	E	S	N
Z	R	F	M	B	U	R	G	R	D	T	I	U	U	D
F	E	W	V	S	B	Q	E	R	S	E	A	I	S	O
O	T	R	E	R	C	B	A	C	O	R	T	T	K	W
M	B	B	A	D	W	L	O	N	B	T	S	V	I	S
I	I	J	W	U	B	K	S	J	O	I	J	L	E	K
O	J	I	G	O	S	L	H	T	O	P	Q	O	F	I
D	D	P	K	V	C	N	P	C	K	Y	S	F	T	C
F	X	S	F	S	V	Z	C	S	G	I	H	I	J	F
I	I	U	V	I	M	M	O	B	I	L	E	R	H	W

EUSEBIO
FORLAN
IMMOBILE
KIEFT
KRANKL
LEWANDOWSKI
MAKAAY
MCCOIST
POLSTER
RUSH
SKOBLAR
SUAREZ
TAYLOR
TONI
TOTTI
ZHEKOV

Find each of the words in the grid of letters. Words may be hidden horizontally, vertically or diagonally and in either a forwards or backwards direction.

Monday **21** — AC Milan

They are no longer the force they once were, but the great team of the late-80s won three Ballons d'Or in a row (Ruud Gullit in 1987 and Marco van Basten in 1988 and 1989).

Tuesday **22** — AC Milan

In fact, in both 1988 and 1989, all three nominees played for Milan! The only team to match this feat are Pep Guardiola's Barcelona of 2010, when Lionel Messi, Andrés Iniesta and Xavi were all nominated.

Wednesday **23** — AC Milan

In 1986, Milan was acquired by the Italian businessman Silvio Berlusconi, who kept control of the club even after he was elected Prime Minister of Italy in 2001. Berlusconi would sell the club in 2017, six years after he left office.

Thursday **24** — UEFA Champions League

In 2024 the Champions League switched to a new format. Instead of being sorted into 8 groups of 4, all 36 teams play in one giant group, but each team only plays against 8 opponents. After those 8 games, the top 8 teams advance straight to the round of 16, the bottom 12 are knocked out, and the rest go to playoffs.

Friday **25** — Sheffield Wednesday

Sheffield Wednesday are one of the oldest football clubs in the world. They were formed in 1867 as an offshoot of The Wednesday Cricket Club, so called because the founding members had a half-day off work on Wednesdays.

Saturday **26** — Kieran Trippier

English full-back Kieran Trippier started his career at Manchester City, but he didn't make a single appearance for the Sky Blues.

Sunday **27** — Kieran Trippier

After impressing in the Championship with Barnsley and Burnley, he became an important part of Mauricio Pochettino's Tottenham team. At the age of 33, he is still a key player for both Newcastle and England.

Argentinian manager:

O A

L E

L A B

M I

C

E R S

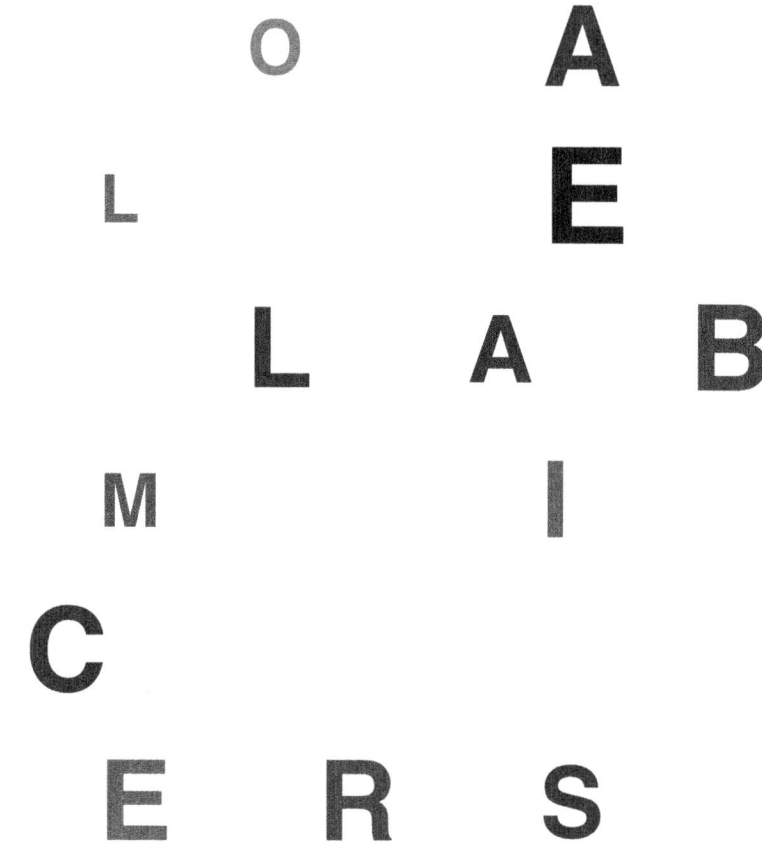

Write your answer on the line below (7,6):

_ _ _ _ _ _ _ _ _ _ _ _ _

Monday **28** Xavi Simons

At the age of just 21, RB Leipzig's Dutch winger Xavi Simons is one of the best players in the Bundesliga. When he was younger he was one of the stars of Barcelona's La Maisia academy – he had a deal with Nike at the age of just 13, and by the time was 16 he had 2 million Instagram followers!

Tuesday **29** José Mourinho

José Mourinho is the only non-Italian coach to be inducted into the Italian Football Hall of Fame during his lifetime.

Wednesday **30** José Mourinho

Between playing football and becoming a professional manager, Mourinho worked as a PE teacher.

Thursday **1** José Mourinho

Didier Drogba joined Chelsea in July 2004, just one month after Mourinho. Both men returned to the club in 2014, when Mourinho was reappointed manager.

Friday **2** José Mourinho

After leaving Chelsea for the second time, José Mourinho became the manager of Manchester United. In a Chelsea – Man U match in 2018, he made the news after losing his temper at a Chelsea coach who ran up to him while celebrating a goal. Mourinho was fined £6,000 for 'improper conduct' by the FA.

Saturday **3** Inter Milan

Inter were formed in 1908 following a disagreement within the Milan Cricket and Football Club (now known as AC Milan) about accepting foreign players.

Sunday **4** Inter Milan

The new club was named Football Club Internazionale (still their official name), because, unlike their parent club, they had no limits on foreigners.

ARGENTINA

2022 World Cup final

Manager: **Lionel Scaloni**

This is Argentina's starting lineup from the 2022 World Cup final. Can you fill in the two missing players?

Monday **5** — Inter Milan

Inter's colours, black and blue stripes with a gold star, are based on the colours of a starry night.

Tuesday **6** — Alex Ferguson

Alex Ferguson was Manchester United manager for 26 years, which is the longest reign in post-war English football history (the longest serving manager of all time was Fred Everiss who managed West Bromwich Albion for almost 46 years, from August 1902 until May 1948!).

Wednesday **7** — Alex Ferguson

During his time at Manchester United, Ferguson won more trophies than any other football manager in history – a staggering 49.

Thursday **8** — FA Cup

In the very first FA Cup final between Royal Engineers and Wanderers in 1872, Engineers player Edmund Cresswell broke his collarbone and refused to leave the pitch, playing the rest of the match in tremendous pain.

Friday **9** — FA Cup

He was outdone in the 1965 final between Liverpool and Leeds United, when Liverpool left-back Gerry Byrne suffered the exact same injury in the third minute. Not only did Byrne play for the full 90, he stayed on for an additional 30 minutes of extra time, and provided an assist for Liverpool's first goal!

Saturday **10** — Ajax

AFC Ajax was founded in Amsterdam in 1900. It was named after the Greek mythological hero Ajax the Great.

Sunday **11** — Ajax

They were perhaps the greatest team in the world in the early 1970s, when manager Rinus Michels and star player Johan Cruyff won three European Cups in a row and invented 'Total Football.'

North London club:

E R

S

A N

A

L

Write your answer on the line below (7):

_ _ _ _ _ _ _

Monday **12** — Ajax

Their only other European Cup came in 1995 under manager Louis van Gaal. That team was one of the most exciting in Europe, and included such players as Edgar Davids, Marc Overmars, Clarence Seedorf, Jari Litmanen and Patrick Kluivert.

Tuesday **13** — Barcelona

Barcelona earned the nickname 'The Dream Team' in the 1980s and 90s, when manager Johan Cruyff brought in great players like Michael Laudrup, Ronald Koeman, Hristo Stoichkov and Pep Guardiola, and played in the Dutch 'Total Football' style.

Wednesday **14** — Barcelona

Guardiola built on Cruyff's foundation when he took over as manager in 2008. His Barcelona team which included Lionel Messi, Sergio Busquets, Xavi and Andrés Iniesta, is considered by many to be the greatest club team of all time.

Thursday **15** — Barcelona

Barcelona are best known for football, but the club also has basketball, volleyball, futsal, rugby and various hockey teams.

Friday **16** — Formations

The football of the 1870s was extremely attacking, which is reflected in the earliest known football formation, which is 1-2-7 – that's one defender, two midfielders and seven forwards!

Saturday **17** — Formations

In their first international match against Scotland, England took it a step further, playing in a 1-1-8 formation!

Sunday **18** — Formations

In the 1880s, the 2-3-5 or 'Pyramid' formation was introduced, and it was used by most teams until the 1930s. It had two defenders (then called 'fullbacks'), three midfielders (then called 'halfbacks'), two wingers, two 'inside forwards' and a centre forward.

Most Expensive Transfers

I	K	R	G	M	M	T	D	R	A	M	Y	E	N	L
T	E	C	R	A	T	P	F	Z	U	O	G	Z	M	M
V	U	O	E	G	E	U	D	K	R	R	X	E	B	J
R	K	U	A	E	A	L	U	Y	I	I	I	D	A	W
L	A	T	L	G	S	A	E	E	T	O	L	N	P	U
W	K	I	I	U	S	C	Z	B	P	H	E	A	P	H
T	U	N	S	M	W	M	A	O	M	Z	F	N	E	A
S	L	H	H	E	A	P	G	I	B	E	I	R	S	Z
D	T	O	E	N	A	B	X	C	C	Q	D	E	T	A
D	T	M	N	T	A	S	P	U	K	E	P	F	A	R
L	T	P	O	R	S	M	V	E	L	A	D	R	Q	D
M	A	H	G	N	I	L	L	E	B	W	V	O	D	E
S	J	U	A	I	A	E	I	A	P	S	A	S	Y	N
R	I	R	I	C	E	F	A	B	Q	T	A	B	I	A
A	O	D	L	A	N	O	R	C	P	E	G	G	C	K

BELLINGHAM
CAICEDO
COUTINHO
DEMBELE
FELIX
FERNANDEZ
GREALISH
GRIEZMANN
HAZARD
KANE
LUKAKU
MBAPPE
NEYMAR
POGBA
RICE
RONALDO

Find each of the words in the grid of letters. Words may be hidden horizontally, vertically or diagonally and in either a forwards or backwards direction.

Monday **19** Formations

In the mid-1920s, following a change in the offside law, Arsenal manager Herbert Chapman invented the 'WM' formation, or 3-2-2-3.

Tuesday **20** Formations

In the WM, one of the 'halfbacks' of the 2-3-5 formation moved back between the two 'fullbacks' to become the 'centre back,' which is why nowadays left-backs and right-backs are referred to as fullbacks.

Wednesday **21** Formations

In the 1950s the Brazillian coach Flávio Costa and the Hungarian Béla Guttman developed the 4-2-4 formation, which was the first to utilise a back four. Among many other teams, the great Brazil team of the 1970 World Cup used this formation.

Thursday **22** Formations

The 4-2-4 evolved into the 4-4-2, which was the most common formation in the 1990s and early 2000s, and is still used by many teams today. It was famously used by Leicester City when they won the Premier League title in 2016.

Friday **23** Formations

The 4-2-4 also evolved into the 4-3-3, which is one of the most popular formations today. It was famously used by the great Netherlands team of the 1970s, and more recently it has been used by Pep Guardiola's Manchester City and Jürgen Klopp's Liverpool.

Saturday **24** Formations

4–6–0 is an unconventional formation in which the centre-forward is replaced by an attacking-midfielder.

Sunday **25** Formations

It was first used by Luciano Spalletti's Roma team in 2005, and it has also been used by Alex Ferguson's Manchester United in 2007/08, and by Vicente del Bosque's Spain team at Euro 2012.

verpool player:

A

A O

L H

S M

Write your answer on the line below (2,5):

_ _   _ _ _ _ _

Monday **26** — FIFA World Cup

In the 2002 FIFA World Cup, Australia beat American Samoa with a final score of 31 - 0.

Tuesday **27** — Cristiano Ronaldo

Cristiano Ronaldo has scored more hat-tricks than any other current player, with over 60 to his name.

Wednesday **28** — Olympic Football

Great Britain won the first Olympic football tournament in 1908.

Thursday **29** — Three Lions

The football anthem 'Three Lions' holds the Guiness World Record for the biggest chart fall in UK history, plummeting straight from number 1 to number 97 in the summer of 2018.

Friday **30** — Oldest Football Stadium

The world's oldest football stadium is Sandygate in South Yorkshire, having opened in 1804. Its home club, Hallam FC, have been playing there since 1860.

Saturday **31** — Ethan Nwaneri

In 2022, Ethan Nwaneri became the youngest ever player to compete in the Premier League, taking to the pitch for Arsenal at the age of just 15.

Sunday **1** — Bradley Walsh

Prior to his career as a television presenter and actor, Bradley Walsh played for Brentford Football Club.

FA Cup Winning Captains

Z	R	N	A	M	E	H	A	G	E	B	R	P	D	I
L	F	O	F	A	X	H	A	E	Y	R	R	E	T	A
H	E	S	A	S	K	T	R	R	K	M	A	O	I	P
P	R	R	K	P	R	A	R	R	I	H	L	A	P	J
R	N	E	L	R	E	K	C	A	S	E	T	R	E	M
S	A	D	T	U	H	U	B	R	R	E	I	V	A	L
H	N	N	O	Z	G	A	S	D	R	S	B	V	L	R
J	D	E	R	A	Z	P	I	L	I	C	U	E	T	A
L	E	H	C	I	E	M	H	C	S	V	B	X	K	T
K	S	D	F	F	T	I	A	P	N	P	H	O	P	T
S	R	L	I	E	Y	T	Z	E	M	E	M	S	E	F
I	O	K	V	N	E	R	X	A	C	P	L	O	D	O
L	N	E	W	T	A	T	C	O	A	Y	M	A	Y	S
M	Z	L	R	V	C	K	P	N	R	S	O	R	V	X
S	E	A	M	A	N	S	Y	I	M	O	W	B	J	P

ARTETA
AZPILICUETA
BOYCE
CAMPBELL
FERNANDES
GERRARD
HENDERSON
JEDINAK
KOMPANY
MERTESACKER
SCHMEICHEL
SEAMAN
TERRY
TEVEZ
VALENCIA
VIEIRA

Find each of the words in the grid of letters. Words may be hidden horizontally, vertically or diagonally and in either a forwards or backwards direction.

Monday **2** — Player of the Century

Diego Maradona and Pelé were joint winners of FIFA's Player of the Century award.

Tuesday **3** — Switzerland

In 2006 Switzerland became the only team ever to get knocked out of the World Cup without conceding a goal. After keeping clean sheets in all three group stage games, they drew 0-0 with Ukraine in the second round and were knocked out on penalties.

Wednesday **4** — Jack Charlton

After the death of legendary manager Jack Charlton, Irish fans gathered on Walkinstown Roundabout to celebrate his life. Charlton had managed Ireland during the 1990 World Cup, when fans had celebrated Ireland's success on the same roundabout.

Thursday **5** — The Russian Linesman

Tofiq Bahramov, the legendary 'Russian linesman' who awarded England a goal in the 1966 World Cup final, was actually from Azerbaijan.

Friday **6** — Leicester City

Leicester City finished 14th in the 2014-2015 Premier League season, but first in the 2015-2016 season – an enormous jump!

Saturday **7** — Spain

Spain is the only country to have won the UEFA European Championship four times, with victories in 1964, 2008, 2012 and 2024.

Sunday **8** — Old Trafford

Old Trafford is the largest club-owned football stadium in the UK, with space for nearly 75,000 people.

Manchester City player:

R H S

A

J L E

K

C G A

I

Write your answer on the line below (4,8):

_ _ _ _ _ _ _ _ _ _ _ _

Monday **9** — Crystal Palace

Crystal Palace FC are named after the Crystal Palace, a glass exhibition hall built in 1851. The palace burned down in 1936, but the football club remains.

Tuesday **10** — The Football War

In 1969, El Salvador and Honduras fought the Football War after El Salvador defeated Honduras in a World Cup qualifier.

Wednesday **11** — Women's FA Cup

The first official Women's FA Cup was held in 2015. Before then, the competition was known as the FA Women's Cup or the WFA Cup.

Thursday **12** — High Altitude Football

In 2007, FIFA banned international matches from being played at more than 2,500 metres above sea level after complaints by Brazilian teams about playing in the Andes. The ban was reversed a year later.

Friday **13** — They Think It's All Over

The famous phrase 'They think it's all over – it is now' was spoken by Kenneth Wolstenhome just as Geoff Hurst scored his hat-trick in the 1996 World Cup Final.

Saturday **14** — Nobby Stiles

Nobby Stiles's first name was Norbert.

Sunday **15** — Cardiff City

As of 2024, only one non-English team has ever won the FA Cup – Cardiff City, in 1927.

FA Cup Winning Teams

S	N	Z	F	B	F	N	S	B	R	E	V	Z	T	I
V	L	O	U	F	I	J	A	U	K	V	S	Y	A	S
Q	K	O	D	G	U	O	K	R	C	E	R	Q	L	C
H	Y	G	O	E	M	P	B	N	N	R	E	Z	L	V
P	T	T	N	P	L	X	Y	L	V	T	R	J	I	D
L	V	U	I	O	K	B	Q	E	R	O	E	F	V	N
O	O	J	O	C	T	C	M	Y	B	N	D	S	N	A
O	H	E	T	M	F	T	A	I	J	G	N	C	O	L
P	O	Z	G	Q	S	F	S	L	W	C	A	P	T	R
R	B	S	T	H	S	T	I	C	B	U	W	H	S	E
E	G	N	T	D	L	D	R	D	O	I	U	T	A	D
V	C	H	E	L	S	E	A	O	R	U	O	P	A	N
I	M	A	H	T	S	E	W	A	P	A	N	B	X	U
L	U	L	A	N	E	S	R	A	B	T	C	T	G	S
B	A	R	N	S	L	E	Y	U	B	U	R	Y	Y	L

ARSENAL
ASTON VILLA
BARNSLEY
BLACKPOOL
BURNLEY
BURY
CARDIFF CITY
CHELSEA
EVERTON
LIVERPOOL
NOTTS COUNTY
PORTSMOUTH
SUNDERLAND
WANDERERS
WEST HAM
WIMBLEDON

Find each of the words in the grid of letters. Words may be hidden horizontally, vertically or diagonally and in either a forwards or backwards direction.

Monday **16** Wanderers FC

Five of the first seven FA Cups were won by Wanderers FC, a team which never had a home stadium – hence the name.

Tuesday **17** Kevin Keegan

Kevin Keegan's nicknames include 'King Kev' and 'Mighty Mouse.'

Wednesday **18** Jules Rimet Trophy

The original FIFA World Cup Trophy, called the Jules Rimet Trophy, was stolen in 1966 and found in a hedge seven days later by a dog called Pickles. However, it was stolen again in 1983 – this time for good.

Thursday **19** West Ham or Aston Villa?

In 2015, then Prime Minister David Cameron made an embarrassing gaffe when he asked a crowd to support West Ham. Cameron had previously said he was an Aston Villa fan, and blamed the mistake on 'brain fade.'

Friday **20** David Beckham

David Beckham was given his middle name, Robert, in tribute to Bobby Charlton.

Saturday **21** Luton Town

One of the main entrances to Luton Town's Kenilworth Road stadium is through a row of terraced houses.

Sunday **22** Pelé

Pelé's real name was Edson Arantes do Nascimento.

Former England goalkeeper:

T R N E

T E S

O

P

H

L I

Write your answer on the line below (5,7):

_ _ _ _ _   _ _ _ _ _ _ _

Monday **23** — Longest Match

The longest football match in history took place in 1946 between Stockport County and Doncaster Rovers, and lasted 3 hours and 23 minutes (before the introduction of penalty shootouts, if a game went longer than 120 minutes, extra time would continue until a goal was scored).

Tuesday **24** — Christmas Truce

In the Christmas Day football match of 1914 – in which British soldiers stopped fighting to play the German Battalion – the score was 2-1 to the Germans.

Wednesday **25** — Peter Shilton

English goalkeeper Peter Shilton currently holds the record for most official matches played, having made over 1400 appearances across the course of his career.

Thursday **26** — Dundee United

Dundee United have won 100% of their games against Barcelona.

Friday **27** — Premier League

Although Scottish managers have claimed the title, the Premier League has yet to be won by an English manager.

Saturday **28** — Red Cards

Mexican referee Arturo Brizio Carter holds the record for the most players sent off during the World Cup, having given away seven red cards. His yellow card record isn't too shabby either: it's 29.

Sunday **29** — Gary Lineker

In 2016, Gary Lineker presented Match of the Day in his underwear after Leicester City won the Premier League.

Can you identify which goalkeeper's glove is at the bottom of the stack?

Monday **30** — Gianluigi Buffon

The goalkeeper with the record for most clean sheets is the Italian former player Gianluigi Buffon, having played an impressive 501 matches without a goal.

Tuesday **1** — Gerardo Bedoya

The Colombian Gerardo Bedoya was the most sent-off player in history, having received a total of 46 red cards over the course of his career.

Wednesday **2** — Longest Goal

The longest distance goal recorded was scored by a League Two goalkeeper from their own six-yard box. The Welsh keeper kicked the ball just over 96 metres to reach the goal.

Thursday **3** — Most Headers

The most headers scored by a player in a single game is 5.

Friday **4** — Pitch Invasion

In 2017, the new Wembley Stadium had its pitch invaded by fans for the first time. Millwall supporters ran onto the pitch after their team defeated Bradford City 1 - 0.

Saturday **5** — Ali Daei

In 2004, Ali Daei became the first male player to score over 100 international goals.

Sunday **6** — Civil Service

The Civil Service has its own football club, which has been around since at least 1863. The club still exists, although they play in the amateur leagues. In 2013, they faced Polytechnic FC in the first ever football match played at Buckingham Palace.

ormer Arsenal and Chelsea player:

Y E C

A

L L

S H O

E

Write your answer on the line below (6,4):

_ _ _ _ _ _ _ _ _ _

Monday 7 — Through the Net

In 1962, Soviet footballer Igor Chislenko scored through the net in a match against Uruguay. The goal was awarded, but the USSR's captain Igor Netto persuaded the referee that it should be discounted - even though it put them in the lead.

Tuesday 8 — Battle of Nuremberg

A 2006 World Cup match between Portugal and the Netherlands became known as the Battle or Massacre of Nuremberg after the referee handed out no fewer than four red cards and 16 yellow cards.

Wednesday 9 — Kazuyoshi Miura

As of 2024, Kazuyoshi Miura is the oldest professional footballer in the world. At the age of 57, he plays for the Japanese club Atletico Suzuka, having started his adult career all the way back in 1986.

Thursday 10 — Frank Lampard

Frank Lampard is Chelsea's all-time top goalscorer, having scored 211 between 2001 and 2014.

Friday 11 — Number 10

Many football legends have worn the number 10 shirt, such as Messi, Ronaldinho, Pele and Kane.

Saturday 12 — Goal Kick

In 1997, Iñigo Arteaga became the first goalkeeper to score with a goal kick in a professional match.

Sunday 13 — Number 0

Players aren't typically allowed to wear just the number 0 on their shirts, but Hicham Zerouali wore it for a season of the Scottish Premier League after being nicknamed 'Zero'.

Football Stadiums

G	L	J	C	O	L	D	T	R	A	F	F	O	R	D
O	E	I	O	W	E	T	U	R	W	L	Y	D	K	I
O	G	S	E	L	H	U	R	S	T	P	A	R	K	E
D	D	A	A	O	Q	L	A	Q	I	O	A	S	G	F
I	I	I	N	A	X	F	F	P	R	P	X	A	A	R
S	R	K	F	K	P	P	L	D	S	P	T	F	X	A
O	B	R	I	W	W	T	N	E	N	T	E	M	S	T
N	D	A	E	E	A	A	M	L	O	E	X	E	W	T
P	R	P	L	L	L	A	S	C	S	O	T	N	E	O
A	O	A	D	L	J	A	N	O	L	A	N	E	M	N
R	F	L	E	T	Y	E	R	S	R	I	I	D	B	P
K	M	L	S	R	V	S	M	I	A	D	J	E	L	A
Z	A	I	T	A	S	X	M	Q	P	A	W	H	E	R
W	T	V	R	O	S	E	Y	S	B	H	S	T	Y	K
C	S	C	M	S	N	T	R	U	O	C	N	A	E	D

ANFIELD
CRAVEN COTTAGE
DEAN COURT
ELLAND ROAD
EMIRATES
FRATTON PARK
GOODISON PARK
MOSS ROSE
OAKWELL
OLD TRAFFORD
SELHURST PARK
ST JAMES' PARK
STAMFORD BRIDGE
THE DEN
VILLA PARK
WEMBLEY

Find each of the words in the grid of letters. Words may be hidden horizontally, vertically or diagonally and in either a forwards or backwards direction.

Monday **14** — Cliffside Stadium

The home stadium of Croatian football club HNK Rijeka is located at the foot of a cliff, only metres from the Adriatic Sea.

Tuesday **15** — FC Porto

The Portuguese football club FC Porto is nicknamed 'Os dragões' (the Dragons) and their stadium is called Estádio do Dragão (the Stadium of the Dragon).

Wednesday **16** — You'll Never Walk Alone

You'll Never Walk Alone is most famous as Liverpool's anthem, but it is also sung by fans of Celtic, Borussia Dortmund, FC Twente, FC Tokyo and Genoa CFC.

Thursday **17** — English Football Hall of Fame

Eric Cantona was the first person from outside the United Kingdom to be inducted into the English Football Hall of Fame, in 2002. The second was Peter Schmeichel in 2003.

Friday **18** — Rio Ferdinand

Rio Ferdinand was scouted by Frank Lampard Sr, the father of the famous midfielder. Rio went on to play for West Ham alongside Lampard Jr.

Saturday **19** — Juventus

Since 1934, at least one player from Juventus has represented Italy at every World Cup – more than any other Italian club.

Sunday **20** — Jamie Vardy

Jamie Vardy, Leicester City's star player in the 2016 Premier League season, started his adult career by playing for Stocksbridge Park Steels. After that, he played for FC Halifax Town and Fleetwood Town before signing on with Leicester.

French football award:

D

A

B L N

O L

R

O

Write your answer on the line below (6,3):

_ _ _ _ _ _   _ _ _

Monday **21** — Gareth Southgate

Former England manager Gareth Southgate helped popularise waistcoats at the 2018 World Cup, with many fans copying his style.

Tuesday **22** — George Weah

George Weah, the president of Liberia from 2018 to 2024, is a former footballer. He played for Monaco while Arsène Wenger was manager, and later won the FA Cup while playing for Chelsea. He was also the first African player to win the Ballon d'Or.

Wednesday **23** — Marc-Vivien Foé

After Marc-Vivien Foé sadly died during a 2003 match between Cameroon and Colombia, Manchester City (the team he was loaned to) retired the number 23 shirt in his honour.

Thursday **24** — Essam El Hadary

In 2018, Essam El Hadary became the oldest footballer to play in the World Cup when he represented Egypt at the age of 45.

Friday **25** — Thierry Henry

Thierry Henry has won the Football Writers' Association Footballer of the Year award three times, which is more than anyone else.

Saturday **26** — Thierry Henry

Henry was also the first to win the award two seasons in a row, an achievement later matched by Cristiano Ronaldo.

Sunday **27** — Neymar

In 2017, Paris Saint-Germain paid €222 million to transfer Neymar from Barcelona. As of 2024, this record hasn't been broken, making Neymar the most expensive player of all time.

Football Words

W	I	N	G	E	R	E	D	A	E	H	R	A	Z	M
X	G	D	E	F	E	N	D	E	R	E	K	S	A	Y
D	B	D	R	A	C	D	E	R	D	W	R	C	O	G
A	R	T	O	Y	O	V	R	L	E	S	S	O	N	O
D	S	A	U	E	E	R	E	F	E	R	F	S	Q	A
U	D	Y	C	A	R	I	Z	W	K	F	H	I	T	L
G	R	T	K	W	F	O	K	Q	S	A	R	U	P	K
L	G	Y	R	D	O	Y	V	I	H	U	J	G	I	E
D	C	E	I	E	R	L	D	X	H	H	O	R	T	E
H	O	M	L	S	K	E	L	T	B	A	W	E	C	P
A	A	W	D	K	Q	I	G	E	L	B	F	G	H	E
K	C	N	Z	H	C	Z	R	K	Y	O	S	A	C	R
U	H	B	V	J	X	A	I	T	U	A	B	N	W	S
C	B	E	Q	W	Z	C	T	L	S	J	M	A	R	V
I	U	A	U	Q	K	U	A	W	O	I	H	M	M	J

COACH
DEFENDER
FOUL
GOAL KICK
GOALKEEPER
HEADER
MANAGER
MIDFIELDER
OFFSIDE
PITCH
RED CARD
REFEREE
STRIKER
TACKLE
WINGER
YELLOW CARD

Find each of the words in the grid of letters. Words may be hidden horizontally, vertically or diagonally and in either a forwards or backwards direction.

Monday **28** — Luis Suárez

In 2014, Luis Suárez was suspended for four months by FIFA for biting Giorgio Chiellini during a World Cup group match and fined approximately £65,000. During his suspension, he was banned from even entering a football stadium.

Tuesday **29** — Plácido Galindo

In 1930, Plácido Galindo became the first player to be sent off during a World Cup match. He didn't receive a red card, however; they weren't introduced until 1970.

Wednesday **30** — First Women's Club

The first women's football club, the British Ladies' Football Club, was founded in 1895 by Nettie J. Honeyball. The BLFC's youngest player, midfielder Daisy Allen, was only 11 years old.

Thursday **31** — Redknapp and Lampard

Harry Redknapp is Frank Lampard's uncle. Redknapp's wife, Sandra, is the sister of Lampard's mother Patricia.

Friday **1** — Roy Hodgson

Former England manager Roy Hodgson is fluent in five languages: English, French, German, Swedish and Italian.

Saturday **2** — Kaká

At least five professional footballers have used the nickname Kaká. The most famous won the Ballon d'Or in 2007.

Sunday **3** — Army FA

The Army Football Association holds a Challenge Cup every year which army-affiliated teams can participate in. The School of Electrical & Mechanical Engineering has the best record, having won eight times.

Football club whose motto is 'Marching On Together':

S E

T

I D U N

D E E

L

Write your answer on the line below (5,6):

_ _ _ _ _   _ _ _ _ _ _

Monday 4 — Ella Toone

In 2023, Manchester United player Ella Toone received a red card for pushing Eveliina Summanen in a game against Tottenham Hotspur. However, her red card was later rescinded and Summanen suspended after being charged with 'simulation' – faking a fall.

Tuesday 5 — Fastest Own Goal

In 1977, Pat Kruse scored what might possibly be the fastest professional own goal ever, knocking the ball into Torquay United's net just eight seconds after the match against Cambridge United began.

Wednesday 6 — Disgrace of Gijón

In 1982, Austria allowed West Germany to win a World Cup group match 1 - 0, since this would ensure both teams progressed to the next stage. This provoked fury in Algeria, whose national team were knocked out as a result, and has come to be known as the Disgrace of Gijón.

Thursday 7 — Zinedine Zidane

Zinedine Zidane retired in 2004, but then returned to captain France in the 2006 World Cup. His leadership helped France to the finals, where they drew 1 - 1 with Italy.

Friday 8 — Zinedine Zidane

The match was decided by a penalty shootout, but Zidane didn't participate; he had been sent off for headbutting Marco Materazzi. Italy won the penalties 5 - 3.

Saturday 9 — Handball

In 2019, the Laws of the Game were changed so that any goal scored by hand was automatically disallowed, even if it was accidental.

Sunday 10 — Golden Boot

Teddy Sheringham was the first footballer to win the Premier League Golden Boot award in 1993. After him, no Tottenham Hotspur player would win the award until Harry Kane in 2016.

French Footballers

I	B	E	S	E	A	M	E	Z	N	E	B	R	H	B
W	M	R	J	J	F	K	J	M	N	A	Z	R	E	R
I	E	P	P	A	B	M	H	T	T	K	F	D	N	W
L	A	A	C	Y	L	L	I	A	S	E	D	P	R	K
T	D	B	R	S	I	B	L	J	K	O	Y	J	Y	Q
O	O	O	G	I	M	A	R	U	H	T	K	P	U	F
R	I	D	N	O	E	R	Z	E	H	T	R	A	B	I
D	I	E	U	N	P	I	M	G	Z	C	B	U	O	I
T	M	S	B	Z	A	V	V	V	I	Z	N	M	W	H
F	R	C	W	J	A	M	A	X	D	R	D	A	M	B
I	B	H	T	E	J	R	Z	U	K	X	O	T	L	N
K	G	A	B	R	A	S	A	E	H	G	X	U	A	B
Q	B	M	W	N	N	R	R	Z	I	H	E	I	D	Y
X	W	P	E	L	O	F	W	K	I	R	R	D	Z	B
J	Z	S	Z	B	D	I	O	P	F	L	G	I	O	Z

BARTHEZ
BENZEMA
BLANC
DESAILLY
DESCHAMPS
GIROUD
GRIEZMANN
HENRY
LIZARAZU
MATUIDI
MBAPPE
POGBA
THURAM
VARANE
VIEIRA
WILTORD

Find each of the words in the grid of letters. Words may be hidden horizontally, vertically or diagonally and in either a forwards or backwards direction.

Monday **11** — Own Goals

In 1994, Barbados deliberately scored an own goal in the last few minutes of their World Cup qualifier against Grenada. Why? In order to qualify, Barbados had to beat Grenada by two goals, but the score was only 2 - 1 in their favour. By scoring the own goal, they forced extra time - and went on to knock Grenada out.

Tuesday **12** — Tallest Player

Simon Bloch Jørgensen might just be the tallest person ever to play professional football. At 6'10" - a staggering 2.10 metres - he towered over all other players on the pitch. At the time of his retirement in 2022, Jørgensen played for the small English club of Waltham Abbey.

Wednesday **13** — Shortest Player

Élton José Xavier Gomes - nicknamed Élton Arábia - is one of the shortest professional football players of all time, at 5'1" or 1.54 metres high. Arábia, a Brazilian, has played for multiple Saudi Arabian clubs - hence the nickname.

Thursday **14** — Paul Gascoigne

Former Newcastle and Tottenham player John Paul Gascoigne - better known as Paul Gascoigne or just Gazza - was named after the Beatles: John for John Lennon, Paul for Paul McCartney.

Friday **15** — Miracle of Istanbul

'The Miracle of Istanbul' refers to the 2005 UEFA Champions League final, in which Liverpool - captained by Steven Gerrard - clawed back Milan's 3 - 0 lead to end the game on a draw, then win via penalties. It was Liverpool's fifth time winning the Champions League, and earned them the right to permanently keep their trophy.

Saturday **16** — WW2

The FA Cup was put on pause during World War Two, but teams competed for the Football League War Cup instead. In spite of the threat from German bombers, over 40,000 people attended the first final at Wembley.

Sunday **17** — UEFA Cup

Tottenham Hotspur were the first winners of the UEFA Cup when the competition started in 1971. The second team to win were also English: Liverpool.

ost recent winners of the World Cup:

R I N

N A

E

T

G

A

Write your answer on the line below (9):

_ _ _ _ _ _ _ _ _

Monday **18** Rogério Ceni

No other goalkeeper has scored as many goals as the Brazilian Rogério Ceni, whose record of 129 is nearly double that of his nearest contender. None of Ceni's goals came from goal kicks, however; they were scored via penalties or free kicks.

Tuesday **19** Andy Murray

As a teenager, Andy Murray was approached by Rangers to train at their youth academy, but he chose instead to focus on tennis, becoming a Wimbledon superstar.

Wednesday **20** Leonardo Bonucci

At 34, Italy's Leonardo Bonucci became the oldest player to score in a Euro final with his goal against England in 2021.

Thursday **21** Fulham and Chelsea

In the early 1900s Fulham were offered the lease of Stamford Bridge but declined. Owner Gus Mears went on to found a new football club to play at the stadium – Chelsea – that would be one of Fulham's main rivals.

Friday **22** Zlatan Ibrahimović

Aged 17, Zlatan Ibrahimović turned down Arsène Wenger's offer of trying out for Arsenal because (in Ibrahimović's own words) 'Zlatan doesn't do auditions.'

Saturday **23** Gareth Bale

Outside of football, Gareth Bale also plays golf at a high level. In 2023, he participated in an American golf tournament as an amateur.

Sunday **24** Own Goals

In 2002, the Madagascan team SO l'Emyrme scored a staggering 149 own goals in protest against a dubious penalty in another match. The winners of the championship had already been decided, so it made no difference if they won or lost.

Can you identify which trophy is at the bottom of the stack?

Monday **25** EA Sports

The bestselling sports video game franchise FIFA was launched in 1993. It released its last instalment, FIFA 23, in 2022, after EA Sports and FIFA (the organisation) did not renew their licensing agreement. However, EA Sports continued to publish football games under the franchise 'EA Sports FC.'

Tuesday **26** Tactical Foul

Giorgio Chiellini – no stranger to being fouled himself – grabbed Bukayo Saka's shirt during the last few minutes of the England - Italy Euros final in 2021, throwing him to the ground. Although Chiellini was given a yellow card, he prevented Saka from getting any closer to the goal in a classic example of a tactical foul.

Wednesday **27** Jerzy Dudek

After retiring from football, Liverpool's star goalie Jerzy Dudek became a racing driver, competing in a racing cup every year from 2013 to 2016.

Thursday **28** Most Attended Match

The 1950 Uruguay versus Brazil World Cup match (which Uruguay won 2 - 1) is the most attended international match of all time, with 173,000 official attendees and possibly 220,000 counting those without tickets.

Friday **29** Transfer Fee

Until 1995, players were not allowed to leave their club and register with a new one without their old club's permission, even if their contract had expired. This 'permission' was usually acquired by paying a transfer fee, and players could be left in limbo if the new club was unwilling to pay it. The practice ended with the European Court of Justice's Bosman ruling, which found that this was contrary to the free movement of workers.

Saturday **30** Australia

The Australian women's national football team are nicknamed 'the Matildas' after Australian folk song 'Waltzing Matilda.' The men's team is nicknamed 'the Socceroos.'

Sunday **31** Hot Dogs

In 1926, Fulham became the first English club to sell hot dogs at their stadium.

Spanish football league:

L

A L A

I G

Write your answer on the line below (2,4):

_ _   _ _ _ _

Monday **1** — Football Rivalries

The North London derby between Tottenham and Arsenal is one of the bitterest rivalries in football, equivalent to the Lazio-Roma rivalry in Italy and Scotland's Rangers versus Celtic.

Tuesday **2** — Ian Wright

Ian Wright released the single 'Do The Right Thing' in 1993 while playing for Arsenal. It was produced by Chris Love, one half of the Pet Shop Boys.

Wednesday **3** — Match of the Day

Match of the Day has been on air longer than any other football TV programme, starting in 1964 with Kenneth Wolstenholme as presenter. Since 1999, Gary Lineker has been the presenter, although he was briefly suspended in 2023 after a Twitter controversy.

Thursday **4** — Look Before You Jump

In 2019, Brazilian footballer Anderson Lopes suffered minor injuries after scoring a goal for his team, Hokkaido Consadole Sapporo. Lopes jumped over the pitch's advertising barrier in celebration, unaware of the large drop on the other side.

Friday **5** — Rio Ferdinand

Rio Ferdinand attempted to become a professional boxer after retiring from football, but was denied a licence by the British Boxing Board of Control in 2018.

Saturday **6** — Chelsea

In 1999, Chelsea became the first British team to have an entirely foreign starting line-up, with no British or Irish players.

Sunday **7** — Mascots

Some World Cups have had official mascots, starting with England's World Cup Willie (a lion) in 1966. The most recent mascot is La'eeb, who represented Qatar 2022.

Goalkeepers

I	S	R	Y	P	H	S	Y	H	A	R	T	U	G	B
Y	W	R	Y	G	A	L	M	N	A	W	E	R	R	U
O	K	Y	C	V	O	L	A	V	P	K	S	M	Z	F
H	A	D	A	E	O	O	N	O	S	S	I	L	A	F
Z	L	N	Y	P	E	R	S	S	J	A	R	H	T	O
J	B	E	L	S	N	I	G	T	I	U	Y	I	U	N
O	O	M	T	E	O	S	N	R	T	V	X	A	Q	J
N	A	R	U	T	P	P	G	K	V	E	P	N	R	E
S	A	E	R	R	A	S	R	E	D	N	A	V	I	V
R	R	U	D	R	F	P	T	C	C	W	E	T	S	B
U	O	U	E	Q	L	E	H	C	I	E	M	H	C	S
C	D	I	S	A	W	V	L	K	R	I	R	T	U	P
Q	N	N	O	S	R	E	D	E	R	R	T	Y	L	L
A	D	E	G	E	A	S	S	U	O	N	U	O	B	B
O	L	X	K	R	X	L	J	O	R	L	J	I	S	R

ALISSON
BOUNOU
BUFFON
COURTOIS
DE GEA
EDERSON
HART
LLORIS
MENDY
NAVAS
NEUER
OBLAK
RAYA
REINA
SCHMEICHEL
VAN DER SAR

Find each of the words in the grid of letters. Words may be hidden horizontally, vertically or diagonally and in either a forwards or backwards direction.

Monday **8** Testimonial Match

A 'testimonial' is a football match in honour of a veteran player, for instance the 2013 testimonial for Steven Gerrard that Liverpool played against Olympiacos. Liverpool won 2 - 0.

Tuesday **9** Prisoner of War

In 1914, Jimmy Hogan, the British coach of the Austrian national team, found himself shut up in a prisoner-of war-camp with the outbreak of World War One. Escaping to Hungary, Hogan coached MTK Budapest until the end of the war, only to be treated as a traitor to his country when he finally returned home.

Wednesday **10** US Women's Football

The United States has consistently been more successful in women's football than men's. Their men's team has qualified for the World Cup 11/22 times, with their best placement being third (in 1930) whereas the women's team has qualified for every World Cup and won 4/9 of them.

Thursday **11** The City Gent

Bradford City A.F.C.'s The City Gent is the oldest fan-published football magazine in the United Kingdom. First published in 1984, it continues to this day.

Friday **12** Banned Gesture

From February 2019 onwards, UEFA players can be given a yellow card for making a 'TV-screen' hand gesture, implying that the referee should consult VAR.

Saturday **13** Mascots

In 2002, Stuart Drummond stood for election as mayor of Hartlepool under the name H'Angus the Monkey, Hartlepool United's official mascot. On being elected, he resigned the mascotship.

Sunday **14** North Korea

North Korea has only qualified for two men's World Cups, 1966 and 2010. In 1966, they reached the second stage – the first Asian team to do – but in 2010 failed to progress past the group stage.

Football club whose motto is Nil Satis Nisi Optimum (Only the best is enough):

E

N T

R

V O

E

Write your answer on the line below (7):

_ _ _ _ _ _ _

Monday **15** — Wolverhampton Wanderers

In 1967, Wolverhampton Wanderers spent a season playing in America under the name 'the Los Angeles Wolves'. Without time to build teams of their own, the organisers of the US's new United Soccer Organisation decided to import European teams wholesale.

Tuesday **16** — Wolverhampton Wanderers

The LA Wolves won the tournament, defeating the Washington Whips - actually Aberdeen - in the play-off match.

Wednesday **17** — Sports Personalities

Bobby Moore was the first footballer to be chosen BBC Sports Personality of the Year, in 1966. The next footballer to be chosen was Paul Gascoigne in 1990.

Thursday **18** — The Football Battalion

Of the 600 members of the WW1 17th Battalion, Middlesex Regiment, over 100 were professional footballers, leading it to be dubbed 'the Football Battalion'.

Friday **19** — The Football Battalion

Among the Battalion was Walter Tull, a Northampton Town player and perhaps the first British Army officer of African descent. Tull was killed in action while on the Western Front.

Saturday **20** — VAR

The VAR - 'video assistant referee' - uses monitors and video software to assist the referee on the pitch. They were first introduced to the Premier League in the 2019-2020 season, but have caused controversy.

Sunday **21** — One Arm

Victorio Casa is the only player with one arm to ever play in the North American Soccer League.

Premier League Golden Boot Winners

V	A	R	D	Y	E	O	M	A	N	E	B	O	Z	A
L	O	N	E	W	O	B	B	V	U	Y	E	K	E	R
R	S	V	S	R	S	H	S	V	U	B	A	A	R	V
J	Y	U	T	P	O	H	E	I	M	X	H	N	A	I
S	T	L	A	S	I	O	E	U	Z	E	Q	E	U	O
A	G	U	E	R	O	L	A	A	N	O	I	S	S	Q
D	K	G	S	O	H	M	L	R	R	G	X	A	K	A
R	O	U	A	F	C	I	Y	I	R	E	M	L	R	R
O	J	R	L	S	K	A	W	F	H	A	R	I	D	O
G	T	E	A	R	B	A	M	P	H	P	U	O	N	N
B	L	A	H	A	S	S	E	L	B	A	I	N	K	A
A	A	A	D	X	G	V	I	A	A	R	L	C	G	L
E	M	A	D	N	A	L	A	A	H	G	J	Y	Y	D
U	J	U	V	A	N	P	E	R	S	I	E	V	R	O
Z	E	I	O	S	E	E	L	T	J	R	U	E	S	B

AGUERO
DROGBA
HAALAND
HASSELBAINK
HENRY
HEUNG-MIN
KANE
MANE
OWEN
PHILLIPS
RONALDO
SALAH
SHEARER
SUAREZ
VAN PERSIE
VARDY

Find each of the words in the grid of letters. Words may be hidden horizontally, vertically or diagonally and in either a forwards or backwards direction.

SEPTEMBER 2025 WEEK 38

Monday **22** — Triple-Edged Sword

The US national team's forward line in the inaugural Women's World Cup (1991) was dubbed 'the Triple-Edged Sword' by the Chinese media. Michelle Akers, Carin Jennings-Gabara and April Heinrichs led their team to victory, together scoring a total of 18 goals.

Tuesday **23** — Paul Pogba

Paul Pogba's older brothers, Florentin and Mathias, have both played for the Guinea national team, while Paul has only ever played for France. According to FIFA rules, players with dual nationality are only allowed to play for the country they represented first.

Wednesday **24** — Red Cards for Managers

Since 2018, managers have been able to receive red cards in Premier League games. Everton's manager Carlo Ancelotti was the first to fall foul of the rule in 2020 when he was sent off for arguing with the referee shortly after the final whistle blew.

Thursday **25** — First Televised Match

The first English football match to be televised was a friendly between Arsenal and Arsenal Reserves. It aired on the BBC in 1937.

Friday **26** — 'Ronaldo' Reagan

Cristiano Ronaldo was named after U.S. President and actor Ronald Reagan, whom his father was a big fan of.

Saturday **27** — Pelé

Pelé is the only player ever to win three World Cups.

Sunday **28** — Neymar

During his appearances for Barcelona, Neymar scored 105 goals in 186 games ame of the World Cup Trophy from 1930 to 1970:

E T R

S E I

L

J M

U

Write your answer on the line below (5,5):

_ _ _ _ _ _ _ _ _ _

Monday **29** Bayern Munich

FC Bayern Munich are the most successful club in German football history, having won a record 33 national titles.

Tuesday **30** Ronaldinho

At the age of 13, while taking on a local team, Ronaldinho once scored 23 goals in one game.

Wednesday **1** First World Cup

The first ever FIFA World Cup, held in 1930, was both hosted and won by Uruguay.

Thursday **2** Powerful Shot

As a child, Gigi Riva delivered a shot so powerful that he inadvertently fractured another child's arm.

Friday **3** Zlatan Ibrahimović

Zlatan Ibrahimović inspired his own verb in French ('zlataner'), and Swedish ('zlatanera'). The word means to dominate/humiliate an oponent, or to play with supreme technical skill. While too new to have entered the official French dictionary, it was included in a Swedish dictionary in 2012.

Saturday **4** Rivalries

According to a 2003 survey by The Football Fans Census, less than half of league clubs were involved in an actual two-way rivalry. Many were in fact one-sided.

Sunday **5** Fulham

Fulham FC's home stadium is Craven Cottage. The original Cottage was built in the 18th century by William Craven, and was located amidst Anne Boleyn's old hunting grounds.

Left-footed Players

A	E	M	A	S	F	O	S	C	R	L	P	D	H	F
R	L	A	V	J	Z	F	H	J	T	W	L	X	E	A
R	A	S	G	I	W	A	A	O	A	N	S	F	L	R
D	B	V	L	O	R	V	A	N	P	E	R	S	I	E
G	I	S	A	L	A	H	M	K	T	G	L	O	R	I
S	P	M	T	U	O	L	A	I	F	O	D	E	N	S
K	M	O	A	R	Z	H	R	L	L	K	A	L	L	Z
O	N	S	A	R	I	V	A	L	D	O	A	L	A	Z
S	I	L	V	A	I	E	D	G	O	C	U	G	A	D
F	Y	M	E	E	P	A	O	I	I	A	B	I	T	U
L	M	R	I	R	W	L	N	W	R	O	S	G	W	I
N	E	B	B	O	R	S	A	N	L	B	W	G	O	J
S	S	D	C	H	I	E	L	L	I	N	I	S	I	A
J	S	G	G	R	M	S	L	S	U	J	O	S	P	R
S	I	S	F	N	F	Q	H	E	S	L	K	N	C	F

BALE
CHARLTON
CHIELLINI
DI MARIA
FODEN
GIGGS
HAGI
MARADONA

MESSI
OZIL
RAUL
RIVALDO
ROBBEN
SALAH
SILVA
VAN PERSIE

Find each of the words in the grid of letters. Words may be hidden horizontally, vertically or diagonally and in either a forwards or backwards direction.

Monday **6** — UEFA Champions League

Carlo Ancelotti is the most successful manager in UEFA Champions League history, having won the trophy a total of five times, and twice more when he was a player.

Tuesday **7** — Neil Warnock

Neil Warnock holds the record for most promotions in English football, having acheived a mighty eight. He also holds the record for most games as a professional manager, with a whopping 1626.

Wednesday **8** — Celebrity Supporters

Hollywood actor Tom Hanks is an avid Aston Villa fan, while Pulp Fiction star, Samuel L. Jackson, is a Liverpool supporter.

Thursday **9** — The Beautiful Game

Football is often called 'the beautiful game.' It's not clear exactly who came up with this phrase, but Pelé made it popular when he published his autobiography, *My Life and the Beautiful Game*, in 1977.

Friday **10** — Nat Lofthouse

The Bolton Wanderers' forward Nat Lofthouse was nicknamed the Lion of Vienna because of a goal he scored in England's 1952 game against Vienna. In the process of scoring, Lofthouse was elbowed and tackled by the goalkeeper, but still hammered it home to secure England a 3 - 2 victory.

Saturday **11** — Millwall

Millwall FC's home stadium is known as The Den. Often associated with hooliganism, the fans are renowned for their terrace chant: 'No one likes us, we don't care.'

Sunday **12** — Lev Yashin

Soviet goalkeeper Lev Yashin was called 'the Black Spider' or 'the Black Panther' because of his distinctive black uniform.

Team managed by Carlo Ancelotti:

L M

E

D I R

A

D R A

Write your answer on the line below (4,6):

_ _ _ _   _ _ _ _ _ _

Monday **13** — Amputee Football

The Amputee Football World Cup is an international tournament for players with missing limbs. The first championship took place in Seattle in 1984, and the most recent one was held in 2024 in Istanbul, with hosts Turkey winning.

Tuesday **14** — Longest Name

Jan Vennegoor of Hesselink, a Dutch striker who played for Celtic and Hull City, is often considered to have the longest surname of any footballer. Imagine trying to fit that on the back of a shirt!

Wednesday **15** — Abandoned Match

The 'Battle of Bramall Lane' is the only English professional football match which has been called off because of a lack of players. It took place between Sheffield United and West Bromwich Albion in 2002. Due to a mixture of injuries, substitutions and red cards, the United side was unable to field the required seven players and the match was abandoned in the 82nd minute.

Thursday **16** — Maradona's Shirt

After the 1986 Argentina – England game, in which Diego Maradona scored his famous 'Hand of God' and 'Goal of the Century' goals, Maradona swapped shirts with England player Steve Hodge. When Hodge put Maradona's shirt up for auction in 2022, it went for over £7,000,000 – the most expensive sports collectable ever sold.

Friday **17** — Brian Clough

Brian Clough is most famous for managing Derby County and Nottingham Forest in the 1960s and '70s, but he also served as Leeds United manager for a very short while. Clough was asked to leave just 44 days into his tenure, having won only one out of six games.

Saturday **18** — Puskás Award

In 2023, Marcin Olesky became the first amputee footballer to win FIFA's Puskás Award for the best goal of the year.

Sunday **19** — Red Bull

Austrian company Red Bull have bought and rebranded several sports teams, including RB Leipsig, formerly known as SSV Markranstädt and the New York Red Bulls, formerly known as the MetroStars.

One-club Players

N	B	M	E	C	P	T	E	K	X	Z	S	E	C	V
O	R	Q	Y	P	B	A	C	U	Z	Z	I	Q	D	E
T	K	Z	G	R	H	A	N	G	U	S	A	I	O	L
L	S	F	R	N	S	A	R	S	T	Y	X	N	C	T
R	I	A	E	P	M	M	M	R	O	O	S	A	O	Z
A	U	H	H	B	A	H	S	M	N	S	L	E	T	R
H	O	V	F	Q	D	F	I	L	O	L	P	H	I	R
C	I	F	G	I	A	P	N	B	A	N	H	E	R	E
H	Z	H	R	A	D	A	L	G	B	S	D	N	U	N
B	A	K	E	R	R	T	H	H	G	E	W	R	P	R
H	A	A	M	O	T	A	V	T	T	T	R	Y	A	Y
R	S	M	M	I	N	T	Y	J	E	F	J	T	M	B
I	R	U	T	C	A	R	R	A	G	H	E	R	K	I
T	T	K	B	J	Z	N	D	J	Z	S	H	S	S	K
L	L	E	D	D	I	L	S	K	P	K	L	L	X	K

ADAMS
ANGUS
BACUZZI
BAKER
BUSH
BYRNE
CALLAGHAN
CARRAGHER
CHARLTON
COHEN
DIXON
HAMMOND
HENRY
HIBBERT
LIDDELL
MORAN

Find each of the words in the grid of letters. Words may be hidden horizontally, vertically or diagonally and in either a forwards or backwards direction.

Monday **20** — Michael Owen

Michael Owen's spectacular goal against Argentina wasn't enough to win England a match played during the 1998 World Cup. Although he put England ahead with a 2 - 1 lead, the Argentinians equalised and won on penalties.

Tuesday **21** — Michael Owen

Owen played himself in a children's television programme which aired in 2001. *Hero to Zero* is the story of Charlie Brice, a schoolboy whose poster of the England footballer comes to life.

Wednesday **22** — Goalkeeper's Privilege

Goalkeepers are allowed to wear hats or caps, although most decide not to. Goalkeepers can also wear tracksuit bottoms instead of shorts, and even facemasks if they wish.

Thursday **23** — The Rest of the World

In 1963, a world team played a national team for the first time to celebrate 100 years of football. The English national team took on FIFA's 'Rest of the World' team, who fielded players from Brazil, Hungary, Germany, Scotland, Spain and many other countries. England won 2 - 1.

Friday **24** — The Rest of the World

FIFA's 'Rest of the World' team – also known as World XI – rode again in 1967, when they defeated Spain 3 - 0. They have played various other games throughout the years, defeating Argentina and Russia but losing twice to Brazil.

Saturday **25** — Neymar

In a 2011 game against Colo Colo, Neymar was sent off for donning a mask of his own face during a goal celebration.

Sunday **26** — Santos FC

On 20 January 1998, Santos FC became the first team in any category in the world to reach the milestone of 10,000 goals. Voted one of the most successful clubs of the 20th century by FIFA, they were relegated in 2023 for the first time in the club's history.

French footballer:

D I D

A N

I E N

Z I

E N

Z E

Write your answer on the line below (8,6):

_ _ _ _ _ _ _ _   _ _ _ _ _ _

Monday **27** — Kepa Arrizabalaga

Kepa Arrizabalaga became the world's most expensive goalkeeper in 2018 when he was transferred to Chelsea for £72 million.

Tuesday **28** — East versus West

Between the division of Germany in 1949 and its reunification in 1990, East and West Germany kept up a fierce football rivalry. West and East German regional clubs frequently met on the field, but their national teams only played one game against each other: a 1974 World Cup group stage match.

Wednesday **29** — East versus West

East Germany won 1 - 0, but both teams progressed; West Germany went on to win the cup while East Germany was knocked out in the second round.

Thursday **30** — Football Songs

'Football Crazy' is the oldest-known song about football. Composed by James Curran in the 1880s, it was originally called 'The Dooley Fitba' Club' and can also be referred to by its Scottish title: 'Fitba' Crazy'.

Friday **31** — Football Songs

'Marching on Together', played and sung at Leeds United's Elland Road stadium, is one of the few club songs specifically written for the club in question. It was recorded by Leeds United team members and fans for the 1972 FA Cup Final.

Saturday **1** — Best-seller

The best-selling Major League Soccer jersey in 2024 was Lionel Messi's Inter Miami jersey.

Sunday **2** — Attendance

A total of 14,960,957 fans attended Premier League games from 2022-2023. With the exception of US events, this was the highest league attendance in the world.

Premier League Managers

P	R	Y	A	I	Y	G	N	O	S	N	I	K	T	A
J	P	C	C	L	C	U	R	B	I	S	H	L	E	Y
G	B	A	I	O	G	F	E	R	G	U	S	O	N	J
P	O	T	N	N	E	N	K	O	B	P	A	G	G	T
O	Y	J	X	K	B	N	X	H	A	P	K	A	F	D
R	A	Y	K	I	D	Z	P	G	O	O	C	L	A	A
O	M	N	J	A	G	E	B	U	H	L	O	O	F	L
Y	O	H	C	Z	U	M	R	O	N	K	N	I	B	G
L	Y	W	E	E	O	L	G	L	I	R	R	D	Y	L
E	E	Z	D	I	L	O	N	C	R	A	A	R	X	I
D	S	G	A	I	I	O	J	P	U	E	W	A	I	S
R	E	G	N	E	W	F	T	E	O	N	Y	U	K	H
F	B	T	E	B	M	P	D	T	M	N	W	G	V	F
J	N	O	S	G	D	O	H	J	I	I	P	Z	A	K
F	Q	A	M	L	W	A	B	W	Z	K	P	F	E	W

ANCELOTTI
ATKINSON
CLOUGH
CURBISHLEY
DALGLISH
FERGUSON
GUARDIOLA
HODGSON
KINNEAR
KLOPP
MOURINHO
MOYES
REDKNAPP
ROYLE
WARNOCK
WENGER

Find each of the words in the grid of letters. Words may be hidden horizontally, vertically or diagonally and in either a forwards or backwards direction.

Monday **3** — Nico Williams

Nico Williams, who scored Spain's first goal in their 2024 Euros victory over England, usually wears a shirt with 'Williams Jr' written on the back. This is because he has an older brother, Iñaki Williams, who also plays for Athletic Bilbao. However, Iñaki appears nationally for Ghana, not Spain.

Tuesday **4** — Scotland and England

Scotland and England first played each other at the Oval – a cricket ground – in 1870. They also played the first official international match in 1872; it ended 0 - 0.

Wednesday **5** — Scottish Managers

Every manager of the Scottish national football team has been Scottish except for Berti Vogts, a German.

Thursday **6** — Pep Guardiola

Guardiola holds the record for most consecutive games won in La Liga, the Bundesliga and the Premier League.

Friday **7** — Counter-pressing

The tactic of *Gegenpressing* (German for 'counter-pressing') is credited to German football coach Ralf Rangnick. It involves responding to a loss of posession by immediately pressing the opposing team.

Saturday **8** — George Best

In 1966, the Portuguese press dubbed George Best 'the fifth Beatle' because of his long hair and flamboyant style.

Sunday **9** — George Best

After his death in 2005, Belfast City Airport was renamed George Best Belfast City Airport to honour him. Best is considered Northern Ireland's greatest player.

BARCELONA

2011 Champions League Final

1
Valdés

2 Alves | 14 Mascherano | 3 Piqué | 22 Abidal

16
Busquets

6 ________ | 8 ________

7 Villa | 10 Messi | 17 Pedro

Manager: **Pep Guardiola**

This is Barcelona's starting lineup from the 2011 Champions League final. Can you fill in the two missing players?

Monday **10** — Laws Of The Game

The FA drew up their first laws of the game in 1863. These had some fairly big differences from the modern game. For instance, there was no crossbar, so goals could be scored at any height. Teams changed end every time a goal was scored, and the offside rule was considerably stricter, with any player ahead of the kicker being treated as offside.

Tuesday **11** — Manchester City

The motto of Manchester City is 'Superbia in Proelio,' meaning 'Pride in battle.'

Wednesday **12** — Ted Lasso

According to press around Ted Lasso, the show was partially inspired by the story of Terry Smith, an American who came to the UK to coach the American football team Manchester Spartans. He went on to manage Chester City, who he was credited with rescuing from bankruptcy. When he took over the club in 1999, he was the only American ever to manage a professional English football team.

Thursday **13** — Norwich City

'On the Ball, City' is possibly the world's oldest football chant (as opposed to a song about football, like 'Football Crazy') still in use at games. Written in the 1890s, it's sung by fans of Norwich City, and ends with the refrain 'Hurrah! We've scored a goal.'

Friday **14** — Fantasy Football

In fantasy football, fans pick a team of players before a season and then score points depending on how well the players did in actual games. Invented in America in 1990, the game really picked up steam in the UK with Frank Skinner and David Baddiel's Fantasy Football League TV show, which ran from 1994 to 1996.

Saturday **15** — Vindaloo

Classic football song 'Vindaloo' was written by Keith Allen, the father of the famous singer Lily Allen and of the actor Alfie Allen, who played Theon Greyjoy in A Game of Thrones.

Sunday **16** — Vindaloo

According to Keith's autobiography, the lyric 'Me and me Mum and me Dad and me Gran' was based on something Alfie said as a child.

Scottish Football Clubs

P	M	S	V	A	K	C	O	N	R	A	M	L	I	K
S	S	O	N	S	T	J	O	H	N	S	T	O	N	E
Q	R	I	T	A	S	R	E	G	N	A	R	W	H	Z
U	L	E	H	H	I	C	M	Y	E	G	Z	J	S	C
E	A	Y	V	I	E	N	I	U	O	N	V	J	V	U
E	Y	T	N	O	B	R	O	T	V	P	L	V	A	L
N	R	N	O	A	R	E	W	E	L	B	J	J	X	M
S	U	U	T	U	B	H	R	E	I	E	N	O	Y	D
P	N	O	S	C	K	E	T	N	L	R	C	S	O	Z
A	I	C	G	E	L	R	R	I	I	L	D	Q	J	Y
R	T	S	N	D	M	P	A	D	A	A	F	R	A	F
K	E	S	I	W	T	L	M	Y	E	R	N	Z	I	K
P	D	O	V	E	E	D	N	U	D	E	V	I	N	A
P	F	R	I	S	T	M	I	R	R	E	N	N	W	L
K	K	R	L	G	U	H	T	A	O	R	B	R	A	R

ABERDEEN
AIRDRIEONIANS
ARBROATH
AYR UNITED
CELTIC
DUNDEE
HIBERNIAN
KILMARNOCK
LIVINGSTON
MOTHERWELL
QUEEN'S PARK
RAITH ROVERS
RANGERS
ROSS COUNTY
ST JOHNSTONE
ST MIRREN

Find each of the words in the grid of letters. Words may be hidden horizontally, vertically or diagonally and in either a forwards or backwards direction.

Monday **17** Nottingham Forest

Nottingham Forest are nicknamed 'the Garibaldi' because of their distinctive red shirts, which are similar to the red shirts worn by the followers of Italian freedom fighter Giuseppe Garibaldi during his campaigns to unify Italy in the nineteenth century.

Tuesday **18** Medieval Football

Medieval football was a much more brutal game than the one we know today. Sometimes called 'mob football', it could involve as many players as each team could field, and matches were often fought between rival villages. In place of the modern football, an inflated pig's bladder was used!

Wednesday **19** Highest Ever Football Match

According to the Guinness Book of Records, the highest football match ever played took place on Mount Kilamanjaro in 2017, 5,714 metres above sea level.

Thursday **20** Golden Glove

Manchester City goalkeepers have won the Golden Glove more often than any other team. The Glove is a Premier League award presented to the goalkeeper with the most clean sheets at the end of a season.

Friday **21** Golden Glove

Man City's first Golden Glove winner was Joe Hart at the end of the 2010-11 season. He won it in 2011-12 and 2012-13 as well.

Saturday **22** Ryan Giggs

As a child, Ryan Giggs was captain of the England Schoolboys team despite both his parents being Welsh. Since he went to school in England, he was eligible for the team.

Sunday **23** Santa Claus

FC Santa Claus is a Finnish football team from Rovaniemi, the capital of Lapland and – according to Finnish folklore – the home of Father Christmas. Appropriately, the team play in red and white.

PUZZLE 47 SILHOUETTE

A

B

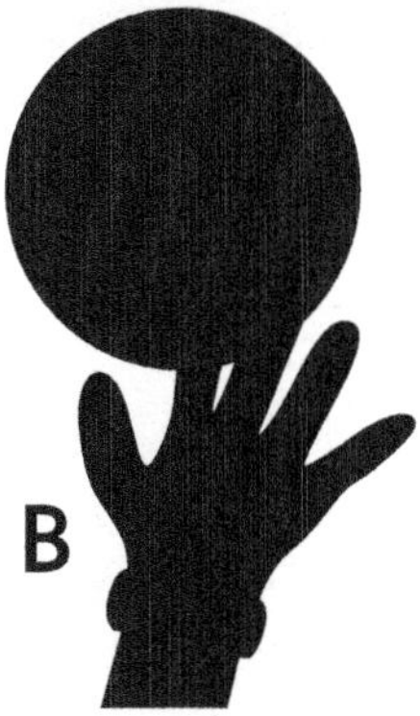

C

D

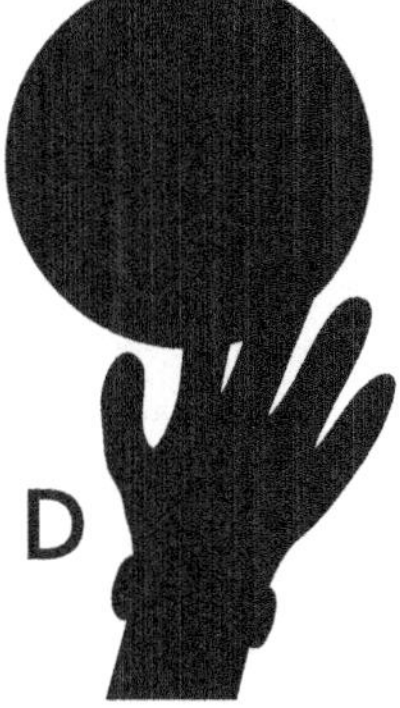

E

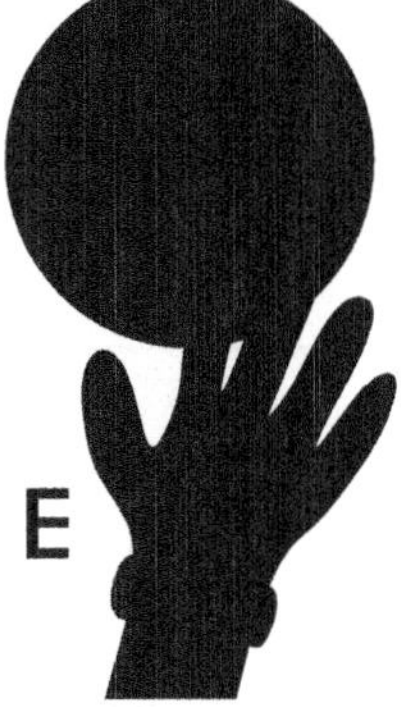

F

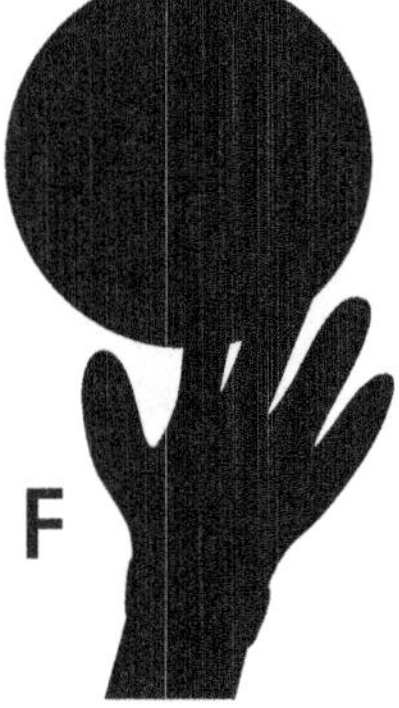

Can you identify which hand perfectly matches the top silhouette?

Monday **24** — Chants

While playing for the Wycombe Wanderers, striker Jermaine Easter was taunted by Bristol Rovers fans chanting 'You're not as good as Christmas!' Despite the teasing, Easter was signed by the Rovers in 2015. No hard feelings, right?

Tuesday **25** — The Great Escape

On the 25th of December 2004, West Bromwich Albion were at the bottom of the Premier League table, but ultimately finished 17th in May, narrowly avoiding relegation. West Bromwich fans refer to this as the 'Great Escape'.

Wednesday **26** — Marcus Rashford

Outside of football, Manchester United striker Marcus Rashford has campaigned against child poverty and for an increase in Universal Credit. He was named *The Guardian*'s Footballer of the Year in 2021.

Thursday **27** — Chants

Fans have come up with many unusual and even self-deprecating ways of taunting their opponents. The chant: 'We lose every week, we lose every week, you're nothing special, we lose every week' is popular amongst many UK football fans, across all football leagues and clubs.

Friday **28** — Tony Hibbert

Midfielder and right-back Tony Hibbert spent his entire career at Everton, making 328 appearances for the club from 2000-2016. Over the course of his career, he did not score a single goal.

Saturday **29** — The Kop

The Kop, a stand in Liverpool's Anfield stadium, is named after the Spion Kop hill in South Africa, where the British and Boers fought a famous battle in 1900. Liverpool's Kop was built in 1906.

Sunday **30** — Vuvuzela

The vuvuzela – a plastic air horn – exploded into global popularity in 2010 during the FIFA World Cup hosted in South Africa. They were banned in all subsequent World Cups due to the barrage of sound.

Tottenham Hotspur Players

Y	U	E	L	D	D	O	H	M	G	X	T	R	O	V
F	E	Z	M	C	C	E	P	E	I	N	I	V	B	C
C	Z	G	D	A	L	Y	B	D	L	F	Z	H	A	H
V	O	W	P	D	H	L	I	W	Z	V	G	A	R	I
M	W	X	D	T	H	G	A	I	E	W	Q	R	C	V
R	U	A	P	B	M	Q	N	N	A	L	Y	W	H	E
A	W	L	H	X	K	I	E	I	N	C	O	A	I	R
T	R	U	L	J	T	S	N	H	R	O	J	P	B	S
N	U	H	G	E	J	T	N	T	D	E	S	M	A	K
Y	I	V	R	Z	R	K	U	W	E	M	H	J	L	C
P	N	G	E	J	P	Y	A	B	I	R	O	S	D	O
R	X	Q	A	K	P	R	V	T	B	N	H	O	Y	M
A	R	E	V	A	D	C	H	F	E	A	Z	X	H	M
T	P	G	E	C	E	V	U	S	H	X	M	M	C	I
T	Z	B	S	K	T	P	T	K	C	W	S	H	S	D

ARCHIBALD
CHIVERS
DIMMOCK
GILZEAN
GREAVES
HODDLE
JONES
MABBUTT
MEDWIN
MINTER
MULLERY
PRATT
SHERINGHAM
SMITH
WADDLE
WOODWARD

Find each of the words in the grid of letters. Words may be hidden horizontally, vertically or diagonally and in either a forwards or backwards direction.

Monday **1** Aston Villa

In 1886, Aston Villa hired the world's first paid footballer manager, George Ramsay. According to the club's advert in the *Birmingham Daily Gazette*, Ramsay would be 'required to devote his whole time to the club,' and in return receive a yearly salary of £100.

Tuesday **2** Real Madrid

Real Madrid' translates to 'Royal Madrid.' King Alfonso XIII of Spain granted them the title and the right to add a crown to their logo in 1920. During the Spanish Republic, they went back to being just plain 'Madrid.'

Wednesday **3** Agony of Mineirão

In 2014, Germany trounced Brazil 7 - 1 in a World Cup semi-final. The match is known as the 'Agony of Mineirão' by Brazilian fans, who were especially embarrassed by the defeat being on their home turf. Germany went on to win the World Cup.

Thursday **4** Preston North End

Lancashire club Preston North End were dubbed 'the Invincibles' after being the first team to win both the top English league and the FA Cup way back in the 1880s. They won the FA Cup again in 1938, but have been relatively unsuccessful since then.

Friday **5** Heart of Midlothian

The Scottish football team Heart of Midlothian might be the only team in the UK which owes its name to a book. They take their name from the Heart of Midlothian mosaic in Edinburgh's Royal Mile, which was made popular by Walter Scott's 1818 novel *The Heart of Midlothian*.

Saturday **6** Andrea Pirlo

Andrea Pirlo has played on both sides of one of the great rivalries in Italian football. He played for Inter Milan from 1998-2001 and AC Milan from 2001-2011.

Sunday **7** Yo-yo Club

Clubs that are constantly being promoted and relegated can be called yo-yo clubs, because they keep going up and down. West Bromwich Albion, Crystal Palace and Sheffield United have all been yo-yo clubs at some point in their histories.

Arsenal player:

O B

K A Y

A U

S K

A

Write your answer on the line below (6,4):

_ _ _ _ _ _ _ _ _ _

Monday **8** Micronation Football

Micronations and unrecognised states have had their own World Cup since 2006. The first VIVA World Cup was held in Occitania (southern France) and the team representing the Sápmi people won.

Tuesday **9** Sealand

The micronation of Sealand - an abandoned oil rig off the coast of Suffolk - had a football team that competed in international games. Their first match was against the Chagos Islands in 2012, although the match had to be held on English soil. The Chagos Islands won 3 -1.

Wednesday **10** Largest Football Stadium

North Korea's Rungrado 1st of May Stadium is the largest football stadium in the world - it can seat over 110,000 people!

Thursday **11** Atlético Madrid

Atlético Madrid are nicknamed 'Los Colchoneros' or 'The Mattress Makers' due to their red and white striped kit resembling traditional mattresses. In the early 20th century, unused red and white cloth from mattress makers made these colours of fabric cheap to come by, and the cloth could easily be converted to football shirts. As a result, the club opted for these colours in 1911.

Friday **12** Scotch Professors

In the late nineteenth century, Scottish players who joined English teams were known as 'Scotch Professors.' At this stage, football was professional - i.e., paid - in England, but in Scotland it was still an amateur sport.

Saturday **13** Amateurs

Glasgow-based Queens Park FC was an amateur club from its founding in 1867 all the way to 2019 - which meant it didn't pay its players! They won the Scottish Cup ten times between 1874 and 1893.

Sunday **14** Hibernian

The Scottish football club Hibernian was founded by Irish Scots in 1875, and proudly features the harp - a symbol of Ireland - on its official logo.

Welsh Footballers

X	K	Y	K	Z	T	C	Z	H	L	W	C	G	Y	U
D	D	M	O	G	B	S	W	Y	D	G	T	M	S	R
Y	O	A	O	L	P	Z	K	I	O	T	I	V	T	F
U	R	L	D	U	F	A	I	O	L	P	D	G	J	U
V	H	L	I	Y	E	L	A	B	O	L	J	P	G	M
G	S	E	K	D	Y	D	R	I	N	R	I	E	V	S
O	E	B	N	L	W	E	W	W	O	N	B	A	N	D
B	I	Y	J	N	X	E	D	H	S	S	S	R	M	D
L	V	W	P	H	E	P	D	S	T	F	E	N	M	S
F	A	K	C	M	K	S	P	G	R	C	N	S	S	J
H	D	F	U	E	L	T	S	P	A	W	O	H	E	R
N	O	D	I	B	B	A	G	E	H	U	J	A	H	K
P	M	L	E	N	H	S	C	C	Y	A	R	W	G	W
F	G	U	N	T	E	R	K	N	E	L	L	A	U	Q
M	L	A	S	L	N	O	S	N	I	B	O	R	H	R

ALLEN
BALE
BELLAMY
BROOKS
DAVIES
EARNSHAW
GABBIDON
GIGGS
GUNTER
HARTSON
HENNESSEY
HUGHES
JONES
ROBINSON
SPEED
WILLIAMS

Find each of the words in the grid of letters. Words may be hidden horizontally, vertically or diagonally and in either a forwards or backwards direction.

Monday **15** — Phoenix Club

When a club goes defunct and is later resurrected, the result is a 'phoenix club.' Strictly speaking, a phoenix isn't a continuation of the old club, but a new one which pays homage to the old. There are two Accrington Stanleys, for example: the original existed from 1891 to 1962, and the successor was founded in 1968 and still exists in the present.

Tuesday **16** — Who Are They?

Accrington Stanley entered the national consciousness in the 1980s, when the Milk Marketing Board used them in an advert. Liverpool striker Ian Rush informs two children that unless they drink their milk, they will never be strong enough to appear for Liverpool – and will have to play for Accrington Stanley instead. The advert popularised the phrase 'Accrington Stanley, who are they?' 'Exactly,' Rush replies.

Wednesday **17** — Sheffield United

Actor Sean Bean and Monty Python member Michael Palin are fans of Sheffield United. The team, nicknamed 'the Blades,' won the FA Cup five times between 1899 and 1925.

Thursday **18** — United of Manchester

In 2005, some Manchester United fans formed the breakaway team FC United of Manchester in protest against the club's new ownership. United of Manchester still exists today and competes in the Northern Premier League.

Friday **19** — Jürgen Klopp

Jürgen Klopp was Liverpool's most successful manager of the 21st century, winning eight major trophies between 2015 and 2024. In his own words, he liked to play 'heavy metal football.'

Saturday **20** — Slang

Football slang varies from continent to continent, with football versus soccer being the most famous example. In North America, for example, they call clean sheets 'shutouts.'

Sunday **21** — Brazil

Brazil is the only country to have featured in every World Cup, with 22 appearances. Germany comes close with 20, followed by Italy and Argentina with 18.

Women's Football

V	O	O	N	M	J	L	O	O	S	O	M	R	E	H
R	O	S	P	R	A	E	L	C	U	I	K	H	Y	M
O	T	S	R	M	E	A	E	B	N	T	T	E	Q	Q
A	J	U	Q	J	K	X	U	X	D	A	N	D	R	V
Y	X	R	Z	N	D	U	L	K	Q	M	U	S	E	R
N	O	S	M	A	I	L	L	I	W	N	J	A	T	E
Y	P	G	H	N	B	P	A	U	B	O	Y	L	W	O
L	A	U	S	H	D	F	R	H	X	B	D	L	L	N
I	T	V	E	I	T	M	A	R	D	W	H	E	H	I
C	M	D	Z	W	N	M	P	Y	V	L	C	T	Q	P
Q	E	S	N	A	M	C	O	U	D	P	A	U	J	A
C	A	X	O	L	J	L	L	T	Z	B	B	P	O	R
N	D	J	R	S	L	M	H	A	L	X	M	A	Y	K
F	U	N	B	H	V	W	E	I	I	R	A	X	D	K
V	J	C	N	Z	P	O	B	O	Z	R	W	Z	V	S

BONMATI
BRONZE
EARPS
HAMM
HERMOSO
KERR
LLOYD
MEAD
PARALLUELO
PUTELLAS
RAPINOE
RUSSO
SINCLAIR
WALSH
WAMBACH
WILLIAMSON

Find each of the words in the grid of letters. Words may be hidden horizontally, vertically or diagonally and in either a forwards or backwards direction.

Monday **22** — Survival Sunday

The final day of the Premier League is known as Survival Sunday, since the matches played on this day decide which teams will stay in the league - and which will be relegated.

Tuesday **23** — Manchester City

Supporters of Manchester City have been known to dance the Poznań. This dance, borrowed from Polish club Lech Poznań, sees the fans place their backs to the pitch and link arms before jumping up and down in waves. It's really quite mesmerising - give it a watch!

Wednesday **24** — Gordon Ramsay

As a boy, Gordon Ramsay played for Rangers. After suffering an injury during training, he dropped out and instead became a chef. In 2008, now a celebrity, he filmed an episode of his The F Word cooking show at their stadium.

Thursday **25** — Antarctic Football

The first recorded football match in Antarctica took place in 1904 during William Speirs Bruce's expedition. Since then, football has continued to be played casually by the scientists studying there, with the various research bases first putting forward teams for a tournament in the 1970s.

Friday **26** — Golden Boys

In 2003, Italian newspaper Tuttosport set up the annual Golden Boy prize for the best young male footballer. Messi, Rooney, Raheem Sterling and Erling Haaland have all been given the prize.

Saturday **27** — Singles

'Good Old Arsenal' is the first charting single released by an English football team; no prizes for guessing which one. Released in 1971, it got to number 16 on the UK Singles Chart and is sung to the tune of Rule Britannia.

Sunday **28** — Footedness

Roughly one sixth of players in the top professional European leagues are 'two-footed,' i.e. capable of playing with both feet. Kevin De Bruyne is an example of this.

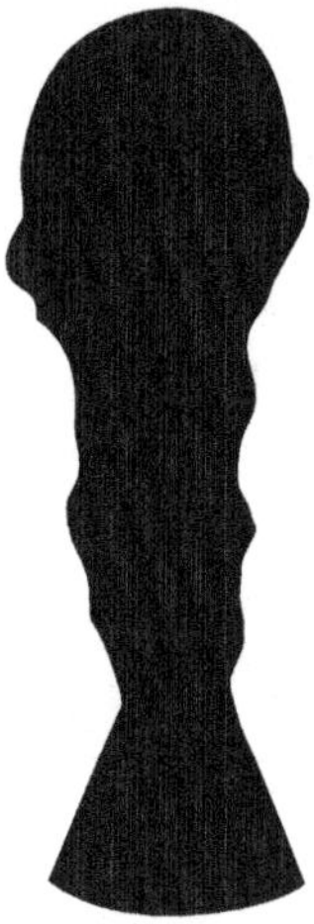

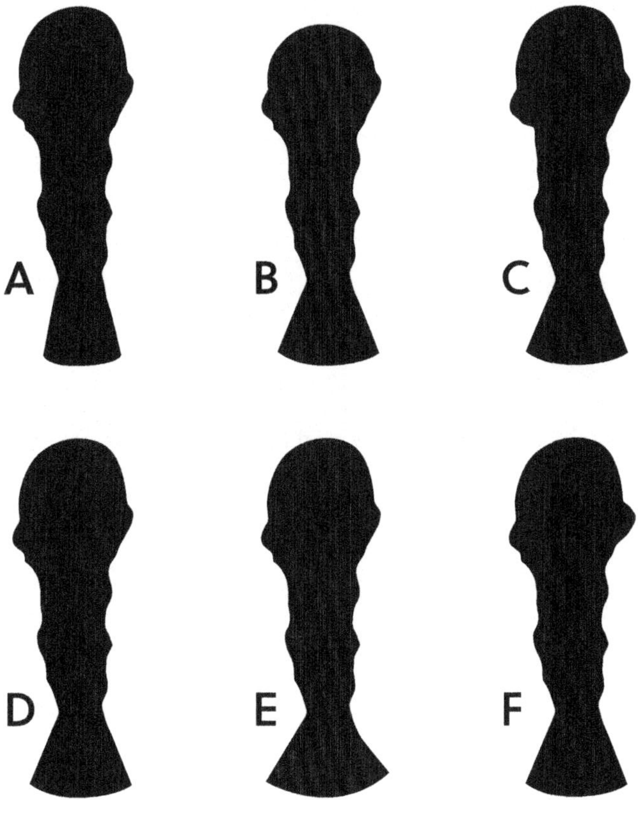

Can you identify which World Cup trophy perfectly matches the top silhouette?

Monday **29** Sergio Agüero

Sergio Agüero earned himself the title of Man City's top goal scorer during his time there from 2011-2021. He was also married to the youngest daughter of footballing legend Diego Maradonna. The couple had a son in 2009 and later divorced in 2012.

Tuesday **30** Social Media

As of 2024, Real Madrid are the most followed football club on Instagram, with 159 million followers.

Wednesday **31** Lionel Messi

In 2011/12, Messi set a record for the most goals ever scored in a single season. He scored an astonishing 73 goals in 60 games!

World Cup Winning Captains

A	M	A	L	L	E	R	A	S	S	A	P	R	T	U
T	E	U	W	U	Y	C	M	S	A	B	S	P	W	K
J	A	R	Y	A	E	V	P	B	E	L	L	I	N	I
W	Z	K	K	W	L	M	S	C	D	Q	R	G	U	O
V	Z	S	R	L	A	T	K	Q	Q	B	M	G	C	W
G	A	V	M	H	L	E	E	G	V	O	O	D	O	K
G	V	S	C	A	N	O	D	R	L	A	O	V	M	A
T	L	S	O	B	T	I	R	C	T	Z	R	Q	B	G
T	E	Z	A	M	P	T	Z	I	D	O	E	E	I	N
D	R	U	L	V	A	S	H	Z	S	F	B	W	L	F
S	E	H	K	B	U	R	A	A	A	F	P	R	H	A
R	L	O	T	R	E	B	L	A	U	S	E	V	M	F
Z	C	T	W	T	S	A	J	E	U	S	A	H	D	H
A	D	V	U	F	L	T	R	N	R	U	T	N	B	W
U	P	Z	P	R	U	H	T	C	A	R	L	O	S	I

ALBERTO
BECKENBAUER
BELLINI
CARLOS
COMBI
DESCHAMPS
LLORIS
MATTHAUS
MEAZZA
MOORE
NASAZZI
PASSARELLA
RAMOS
VARELA
WALTER
ZOFF

Find each of the words in the grid of letters. Words may be hidden horizontally, vertically or diagonally and in either a forwards or backwards direction.

Solution 1

Rice

Bellingham

Solution 2

JOHN TERRY

Solution 3

Solution 4

ERIK TEN HAG

Solution 5

A	S	R	E	P	U	A	E	S	L	E	H	C	M	K
C	R	B	O	S	Z	E	J	C	L	B	E	A	I	F
I	E	H	M	V	S	L	O	U	R	P	R	A	I	U
F	A	A	C	E	S	L	O	O	V	S	X	N	A	O
N	L	E	A	I	T	R	B	O	E	E	T	A	R	Z
E	L	T	P	N	N	M	E	I	P	E	N	E	J	F
B	I	L	I	D	Q	U	L	G	R	R	A	T	E	A
S	V	C	V	H	S	L	M	M	R	L	E	Y	U	S
A	N	E	P	O	E	E	I	N	M	U	E	V	U	S
L	O	L	N	V	I	L	D	A	R	N	B	R	I	O
K	T	T	O	E	A	U	D	S	O	E	N	M	T	L
L	S	I	T	N	D	R	M	O	X	V	Y	E	A	J
J	A	C	R	Q	I	S	R	U	R	Q	D	A	B	H
S	P	U	O	D	F	D	E	C	Y	P	R	Q	B	O
R	O	E	P	O	L	B	A	R	C	E	L	O	N	A

Solution 6

LUKA MODRIĆ

Solution 7

Solution 8

S	L	K	F	J	I	J	E	G	U	N	N	E	R	S
E	E	H	U	T	B	O	R	O	W	S	R	R	O	A
U	V	I	R	B	M	E	Q	H	N	V	O	T	J	H
L	R	R	R	L	V	R	R	P	S	M	Y	U	L	O
B	S	R	R	A	G	H	H	H	A	B	A	Z	S	O
T	R	E	S	D	N	Y	O	G	V	T	L	E	H	P
S	E	D	R	E	E	A	P	I	H	A	S	T	P	S
A	G	D	E	S	H	I	C	L	P	M	W	O	P	L
E	A	E	T	E	E	R	T	W	O	A	E	Z	O	F
M	T	V	T	S	B	L	A	C	K	C	A	T	S	O
P	T	I	A	T	H	A	S	J	N	P	I	J	E	X
C	O	L	H	B	S	R	L	I	T	A	C	U	L	E
Z	C	S	C	Q	E	R	O	B	I	N	S	I	Y	S
U	P	Y	V	T	W	H	I	T	E	S	Z	W	U	A
L	U	D	I	A	L	L	I	V	Q	I	I	A	C	T

Solution 10

DECLAN RICE

Solution 11

P	S	A	K	O	Q	E	H	E	O	R	R	E	I	H
N	E	E	K	F	B	G	A	K	A	I	H	O	S	J
E	P	P	R	I	D	L	N	V	R	V	A	Y	J	O
S	K	W	E	G	N	E	C	E	I	B	D	V	V	F
L	A	N	F	U	I	H	T	S	A	J	A	I	C	Y
O	H	U	E	E	H	N	Z	H	D	F	R	S	M	I
O	S	S	Q	R	S	G	H	Y	L	R	T	N	N	O
B	X	C	F	O	Y	Z	E	O	A	M	I	I	R	W
P	J	I	V	A	L	R	U	N	M	V	D	X	A	B
U	L	R	Q	S	V	F	E	F	V	L	Z	U	I	R
Y	U	E	H	N	I	B	K	H	A	H	O	F	G	P
O	I	A	E	H	N	C	X	M	Z	D	I	A	V	I
L	Z	Q	C	X	H	K	A	R	C	X	S	C	F	Q
W	C	U	I	W	O	C	A	L	O	R	A	P	G	U
Q	B	A	R	E	S	I	N	E	V	H	P	C	H	E

Solution 12

RODRI

Solution 13

R	N	S	U	R	O	T	U	H	F	N	A	Y	W	C
M	X	S	T	I	Y	R	D	E	O	T	R	E	E	N
N	A	G	E	E	K	G	T	S	R	M	D	I	L	O
M	L	B	L	P	T	A	S	R	O	C	T	V	D	S
O	R	K	P	A	G	K	U	Y	S	C	K	E	D	B
I	E	O	Y	H	I	F	E	O	T	L	U	R	O	O
D	U	L	T	R	R	S	H	S	O	A	R	P	H	R
Y	O	U	E	Z	M	E	C	Y	D	R	A	L	L	A
R	O	Y	E	A	T	U	G	F	E	E	E	T	W	V
S	F	I	R	W	I	I	H	N	R	N	D	A	T	L
U	N	O	S	G	D	O	H	R	E	C	R	A	E	P
G	R	E	E	N	W	O	O	D	V	V	O	B	Q	A
O	R	Z	C	A	P	E	L	L	O	U	R	P	S	X
P	M	O	T	T	O	B	R	E	T	N	I	W	C	S
W	K	P	T	V	E	N	A	B	L	E	S	L	S	L

Solution 14

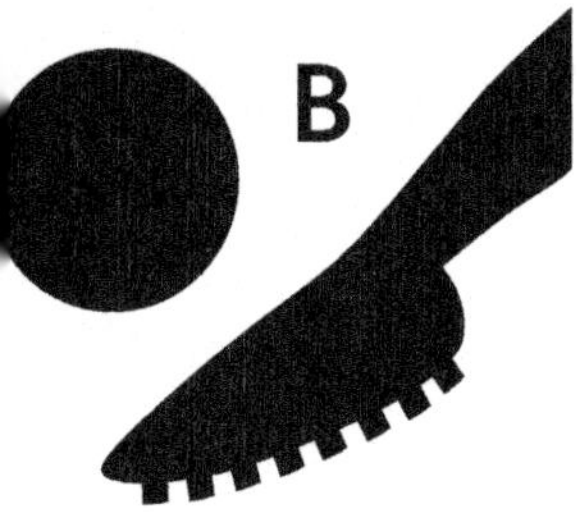

Solution 15

EDERSON

Solution 16

M	I	M	P	V	O	K	E	H	Z	S	N	F	Z	U
A	T	N	B	O	V	E	N	K	Q	D	H	V	T	L
K	S	A	L	K	N	A	R	K	W	P	L	R	N	E
A	H	L	Y	B	I	M	Z	B	M	O	U	D	C	W
A	S	R	L	L	I	N	O	T	H	L	C	R	G	A
Y	U	O	S	W	O	E	E	I	K	S	W	E	S	N
Z	R	F	M	B	U	R	G	R	D	T	I	U	U	D
F	E	W	V	S	B	Q	E	R	S	E	A	I	S	O
O	T	R	E	R	C	B	A	C	O	R	T	T	K	W
M	B	B	A	D	W	L	O	N	B	T	S	V	I	S
I	I	J	W	U	B	K	S	J	O	I	J	L	E	K
O	J	I	G	O	S	L	H	T	O	P	Q	O	F	I
D	D	P	K	V	C	N	P	C	K	Y	S	F	T	C
F	X	S	F	S	V	Z	C	S	G	I	H	I	J	F
I	I	U	V	I	M	M	O	B	I	L	E	R	H	W

Solution 17

MARCELO BIELSA

Solution 18

Mac Allister

Messi

Solution 19

ARSENAL

Solution 20

K	R	G	M	M	T	D	R	A	M	Y	E	N	L
E	C	R	A	T	P	F	Z	U	O	G	Z	M	M
U	O	E	G	E	U	D	K	R	R	X	E	B	J
K	U	A	E	A	L	U	Y	I	I	I	D	A	W
A	T	L	G	S	A	E	E	T	O	L	N	P	U
K	I	I	U	S	C	Z	B	P	H	E	A	P	H
U	N	S	M	W	M	A	O	M	Z	F	N	E	A
L	H	H	E	A	P	G	I	B	E	I	R	S	Z
T	O	E	N	A	B	X	C	C	Q	D	E	T	A
T	M	N	T	A	S	P	U	K	E	P	F	A	R
T	P	O	R	S	M	V	E	L	A	D	R	Q	D
A	H	G	N	I	L	L	E	B	W	V	O	D	E
J	U	A	I	A	E	I	A	P	S	A	S	Y	N
I	R	I	C	E	F	A	B	Q	T	A	B	I	A
O	D	L	A	N	O	R	C	P	E	G	G	C	K

Solution 21

MO SALAH

Solution 22

Z	R	N	A	M	E	H	A	G	E	B	R	P	D	I
L	F	O	F	A	X	H	A	E	Y	R	R	E	T	A
H	E	S	A	S	K	T	R	R	K	M	A	O	I	P
P	R	R	K	P	R	A	R	R	I	H	L	A	P	J
R	N	E	L	R	E	K	C	A	S	E	T	R	E	M
S	A	D	T	U	H	U	B	R	R	E	I	V	A	L
H	N	N	O	Z	G	A	S	D	R	S	B	V	L	R
J	D	E	R	A	Z	P	I	L	I	C	U	E	T	A
L	E	H	C	I	E	M	H	C	S	V	B	X	K	T
K	S	D	F	F	T	I	A	P	N	P	H	O	P	T
S	R	L	I	E	Y	T	Z	E	M	E	M	S	E	F
I	O	K	V	N	E	R	X	A	C	P	L	O	D	O
L	N	E	W	T	A	T	C	O	A	Y	M	A	Y	S
M	Z	L	R	V	C	K	P	N	R	S	O	R	V	X
S	E	A	M	A	N	S	Y	I	M	O	W	B	J	P

Solution 23

JACK GREALISH

Solution 24

S	N	Z	F	B	F	N	S	B	R	E	V	Z	T	I
V	L	O	U	F	I	J	A	U	K	V	S	Y	A	S
Q	K	O	D	G	U	O	K	R	C	E	R	Q	L	C
H	Y	G	O	E	M	P	B	N	N	R	E	Z	L	V
P	T	T	N	P	L	X	Y	L	V	T	R	J	I	D
L	V	U	I	O	K	B	Q	E	R	O	E	F	V	N
O	O	J	O	C	T	C	M	Y	B	N	D	S	N	A
O	H	E	T	M	F	T	A	I	J	G	N	C	O	L
P	O	Z	G	Q	S	F	S	L	W	C	A	P	T	R
R	B	S	T	H	S	T	I	C	B	U	W	H	S	E
E	G	N	T	D	L	D	R	D	O	I	U	T	A	D
V	C	H	E	L	S	E	A	O	R	U	O	P	A	N
I	M	A	H	T	S	E	W	A	P	A	N	B	X	U
L	U	L	A	N	E	S	R	A	B	T	C	T	G	S
B	A	R	N	S	L	E	Y	U	B	U	R	Y	Y	L

Solution 25

PETER SHILTON

Solution 26

Solution 27

ASHLEY COLE

Solution 28

G	L	J	C	O	L	D	T	R	A	F	F	O	R
O	E	I	O	W	E	T	U	R	W	L	Y	D	K
O	G	S	E	L	H	U	R	S	T	P	A	R	K
D	D	A	A	O	Q	L	A	Q	I	O	A	S	G
I	I	I	N	A	X	F	F	P	R	P	X	A	A
S	R	K	F	K	P	P	L	D	S	P	T	F	X
O	B	R	I	W	W	T	N	E	N	T	E	M	S
N	D	A	E	E	A	A	M	L	O	E	X	E	W
P	R	P	L	L	L	A	S	C	S	O	T	N	E
A	O	A	D	L	J	A	N	O	L	A	N	E	M
R	F	L	E	T	Y	E	R	S	R	I	I	D	B
K	M	L	S	R	V	S	M	I	A	D	J	E	L
Z	A	I	T	A	S	X	M	Q	P	A	W	H	E
W	T	V	R	O	S	E	Y	S	B	H	S	T	Y
C	S	C	M	S	N	T	R	U	O	C	N	A	E

Solution 29

BALLON D'OR

Solution 30

W	I	N	G	E	R	E	D	A	E	H	R	A	Z	M
X	G	D	E	F	E	N	D	E	R	E	K	S	A	Y
D	B	D	R	A	C	D	E	R	D	W	R	C	O	G
A	R	T	O	Y	O	V	R	L	E	S	S	O	N	O
D	S	A	U	E	E	R	E	F	E	R	F	S	Q	A
U	D	Y	C	A	R	I	Z	W	K	F	H	I	T	L
G	R	T	K	W	F	O	K	Q	S	A	R	U	P	K
L	G	Y	R	D	O	Y	V	I	H	U	J	G	I	E
D	C	E	I	E	R	L	D	X	H	H	O	R	T	E
H	O	M	L	S	K	E	L	T	B	A	W	E	C	P
A	A	W	D	K	Q	I	G	E	L	B	F	G	H	E
K	C	N	Z	H	C	Z	R	K	Y	O	S	A	C	R
U	H	B	V	J	X	A	I	T	U	A	B	N	W	S
C	B	E	Q	W	Z	C	T	L	S	J	M	A	R	V
I	U	A	U	Q	K	U	A	W	O	I	H	M	M	J

Solution 31

LEEDS UNITED

Solution 32

I	B	E	S	E	A	M	E	Z	N	E	B	R	H	B
W	M	R	J	J	F	K	J	M	N	A	Z	R	E	R
I	E	P	P	A	B	M	H	T	T	K	F	D	N	W
L	A	A	C	Y	L	L	I	A	S	E	D	P	R	K
T	D	B	R	S	I	B	L	J	K	O	Y	J	Y	Q
O	O	O	G	I	M	A	R	U	H	T	K	P	U	F
R	I	D	N	O	E	R	Z	E	H	T	R	A	B	I
D	I	E	U	N	P	I	M	G	Z	C	B	U	O	I
T	M	S	B	Z	A	V	V	V	I	Z	N	M	W	H
F	R	C	W	J	A	M	A	X	D	R	D	A	M	B
I	B	H	T	E	J	R	Z	U	K	X	O	T	L	N
K	G	A	B	R	A	S	A	E	H	G	X	U	A	B
Q	B	M	W	N	N	R	R	Z	I	H	E	I	D	Y
X	W	P	E	L	O	F	W	K	I	R	R	D	Z	B
J	Z	S	Z	B	D	I	O	P	F	L	G	I	O	Z

Solution 33

ARGENTINA

Solution 34

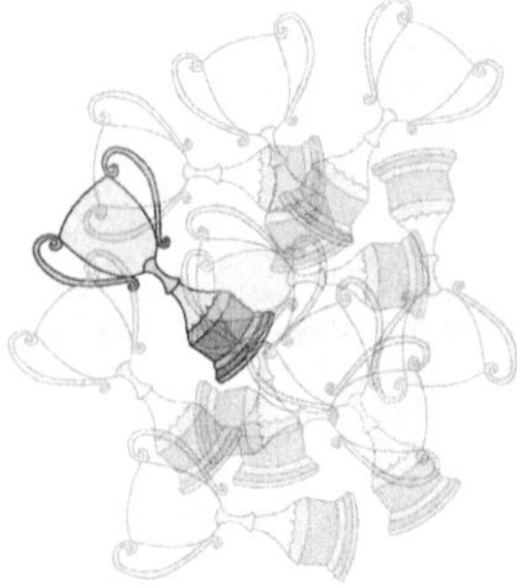

Solution 35

LA LIGA

Solution 36

I	S	R	Y	P	H	S	Y	H	A	R	T	U	G	B
Y	W	R	Y	G	A	L	M	N	A	W	E	R	R	U
O	K	Y	C	V	O	L	A	V	P	K	S	M	Z	F
H	A	D	A	E	O	O	N	O	S	S	I	L	A	F
Z	L	N	Y	P	E	R	S	S	J	A	R	H	T	O
J	B	E	L	S	N	I	G	T	I	U	Y	I	U	N
O	O	M	T	E	O	S	N	R	T	V	X	A	Q	J
N	A	R	U	T	P	P	G	K	V	E	P	N	R	E
S	A	E	R	R	A	S	R	E	D	N	A	V	I	V
R	R	U	D	R	F	P	T	C	C	W	E	T	S	B
U	O	U	E	Q	L	E	H	C	I	E	M	H	C	S
C	D	I	S	A	W	V	L	K	R	I	R	T	U	P
Q	N	N	O	S	R	E	D	E	R	R	T	Y	L	L
A	D	E	G	E	A	S	S	U	O	N	U	O	B	B
O	L	X	K	R	X	L	J	O	R	L	J	I	S	R

Solution 37

EVERTON

Solution 38

V	A	R	D	Y	E	O	M	A	N	E	B	O	Z	A
L	O	N	E	W	O	B	B	V	U	Y	E	K	E	R
R	S	V	S	R	S	H	S	V	U	B	A	A	R	V
J	Y	U	T	P	O	H	E	I	M	X	H	N	A	I
S	T	L	A	S	I	O	E	U	Z	E	Q	E	U	O
A	G	U	E	R	O	L	A	A	N	O	I	S	S	Q
D	K	G	S	O	H	M	L	R	R	G	X	A	K	A
R	O	U	A	F	C	I	Y	I	R	E	M	L	R	R
O	J	R	L	S	K	A	W	F	H	A	R	I	D	O
G	T	E	A	R	B	A	M	P	H	P	U	O	N	N
B	L	A	H	A	S	S	E	L	B	A	I	N	K	A
A	A	A	D	X	G	V	I	A	A	R	L	C	G	L
E	M	A	D	N	A	L	A	A	H	G	J	Y	Y	D
U	J	U	V	A	N	P	E	R	S	I	E	V	R	O
Z	E	I	O	S	E	E	L	T	J	R	U	E	S	B

Solution 39

JULES RIMET

Solution 40

A	E	M	A	S	F	O	S	C	R	L	P	D	H	F
R	L	A	V	J	Z	F	H	J	T	W	L	X	E	A
R	A	S	G	I	W	A	A	O	A	N	S	F	L	R
D	B	V	L	O	R	V	A	N	P	E	R	S	I	E
G	I	S	A	L	A	H	M	K	T	G	L	O	R	I
S	P	M	T	U	O	L	A	I	F	O	D	E	N	S
K	M	O	A	R	Z	H	R	L	L	K	A	L	L	Z
O	N	S	A	R	I	V	A	L	D	O	A	L	A	Z
S	I	L	V	A	I	E	D	G	O	C	U	G	A	D
F	Y	M	E	E	P	A	O	I	I	A	B	I	T	U
L	M	R	I	R	W	L	N	W	R	O	S	G	W	I
N	E	B	B	O	R	S	A	N	L	B	W	G	O	J
S	S	D	C	H	I	E	L	L	I	N	I	S	I	A
J	S	G	G	R	M	S	L	S	U	J	O	S	P	R
S	I	S	F	N	F	Q	H	E	S	L	K	N	C	F

Solution 41

REAL MADRID

Solution 42

N	B	M	E	C	P	T	E	K	X	Z	S	E	C	V
O	R	Q	Y	P	B	A	C	U	Z	Z	I	Q	D	E
T	K	Z	G	R	H	A	N	G	U	S	A	I	O	L
L	S	F	R	N	S	A	R	S	T	Y	X	N	C	T
R	I	A	E	P	M	M	M	R	O	O	S	A	O	Z
A	U	H	H	B	A	H	S	M	N	S	L	E	T	R
H	O	V	F	Q	D	F	I	L	O	L	P	H	I	R
C	I	F	G	I	A	P	N	B	A	N	H	E	R	E
H	Z	H	R	A	D	A	L	G	B	S	D	N	U	N
B	A	K	E	R	R	T	H	H	G	E	W	R	P	R
H	A	A	M	O	T	A	V	T	T	T	R	Y	A	Y
R	S	M	M	I	N	T	Y	J	E	F	J	T	M	B
I	R	U	T	C	A	R	R	A	G	H	E	R	K	I
T	T	K	B	J	Z	N	D	J	Z	S	H	S	S	K
L	L	E	D	D	I	L	S	K	P	K	L	L	X	K

Solution 43

ZINEDINE ZIDANE

Solution 44

P	R	Y	A	I	Y	G	N	O	S	N	I	K	T	A
J	P	C	C	L	C	U	R	B	I	S	H	L	E	Y
G	B	A	I	O	G	F	E	R	G	U	S	O	N	J
P	O	T	N	N	E	N	K	O	B	P	A	G	G	T
O	Y	J	X	K	B	N	X	H	A	P	K	A	F	D
R	A	Y	K	I	D	Z	P	G	O	O	C	L	A	A
O	M	N	J	A	G	E	B	U	H	L	O	O	F	L
Y	O	H	C	Z	U	M	R	O	N	K	N	I	B	G
L	Y	W	E	E	O	L	G	L	I	R	R	D	Y	L
E	E	Z	D	I	L	O	N	C	R	A	A	R	X	I
D	S	G	A	I	I	O	J	P	U	E	W	A	I	S
R	E	G	N	E	W	F	T	E	O	N	Y	U	K	H
F	B	T	E	B	M	P	D	T	M	N	W	G	V	F
J	N	O	S	G	D	O	H	J	I	I	P	Z	A	K
F	Q	A	M	L	W	A	B	W	Z	K	P	F	E	W

Solution 45

Iniesta

Xavi

Solution 46

P	M	S	V	A	K	C	O	N	R	A	M	L	I	K
S	S	O	N	S	T	J	O	H	N	S	T	O	N	E
Q	R	I	T	A	S	R	E	G	N	A	R	W	H	Z
U	L	E	H	H	I	C	M	Y	E	G	Z	J	S	C
E	A	Y	V	I	E	N	I	U	O	N	V	J	V	U
E	Y	T	N	O	B	R	O	T	V	P	L	V	A	L
N	R	N	O	A	R	E	W	E	L	B	J	J	X	M
S	U	U	T	U	B	H	R	E	I	E	N	O	Y	D
P	N	O	S	C	K	E	T	N	L	R	C	S	O	Z
A	I	C	G	E	L	R	R	I	I	L	D	Q	J	Y
R	T	S	N	D	M	P	A	D	A	A	F	R	A	F
K	E	S	I	W	T	L	M	Y	E	R	N	Z	I	K
P	D	O	V	E	E	D	N	U	D	E	V	I	N	A
P	F	R	I	S	T	M	I	R	R	E	N	N	W	L
K	K	R	L	G	U	H	T	A	O	R	B	R	A	R

Solution 47

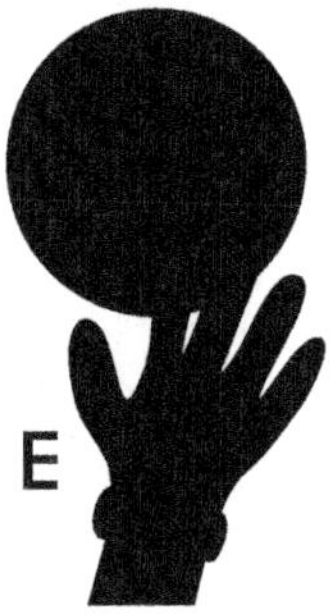

Solution 48

Y	U	E	L	D	D	O	H	M	G	X	T	R	O	V
F	E	Z	M	C	C	E	P	E	I	N	I	V	B	C
C	Z	G	D	A	L	Y	B	D	L	F	Z	H	A	H
V	O	W	P	D	H	L	I	W	Z	V	G	A	R	I
M	W	X	D	T	H	G	A	I	E	W	Q	R	C	V
R	U	A	P	B	M	Q	N	N	A	L	Y	W	H	E
A	W	L	H	X	K	I	E	I	N	C	O	A	I	R
T	R	U	L	J	T	S	N	H	R	O	J	P	B	S
N	U	H	G	E	J	T	N	T	D	E	S	M	A	K
Y	I	V	R	Z	R	K	U	W	E	M	H	J	L	C
P	N	G	E	J	P	Y	A	B	I	R	O	S	D	O
R	X	Q	A	K	P	R	V	T	B	N	H	O	Y	M
A	R	E	V	A	D	C	H	F	E	A	Z	X	H	M
T	P	G	E	C	E	V	U	S	H	X	M	M	C	I
T	Z	B	S	K	T	P	T	K	C	W	S	H	S	D

Solution 49

BUKAYO SAKA

Solution 50

X	K	Y	K	Z	T	C	Z	H	L	W	Ç	G	Y	U
D	D	M	O	G	B	S	W	Y	D	G	T	M	S	R
Y	O	A	O	L	P	Z	K	I	O	T	I	V	T	F
U	R	L	D	U	F	A	I	O	L	P	D	G	J	U
V	H	L	I	Y	E	L	A	B	O	L	J	P	G	M
G	S	E	K	D	Y	D	R	I	N	R	I	E	V	S
O	E	B	N	L	W	E	W	W	O	N	B	A	N	D
B	I	Y	J	N	X	E	D	H	S	S	S	R	M	D
L	V	W	P	H	E	P	D	S	T	F	E	N	M	S
F	A	K	C	M	K	S	P	G	R	C	N	S	S	J
H	D	F	U	E	L	T	S	P	A	W	O	H	E	R
N	O	D	I	B	B	A	G	E	H	U	J	A	H	K
P	M	L	E	N	H	S	C	C	Y	A	R	W	G	W
F	G	U	N	T	E	R	K	N	E	L	L	A	U	Q
M	L	A	S	L	N	O	S	N	I	B	O	R	H	R

Solution 51

V	O	O	N	M	J	L	O	O	S	O	M	R	E	H
R	O	S	P	R	A	E	L	C	U	I	K	H	Y	M
O	T	S	R	M	E	A	E	B	N	T	T	E	Q	Q
A	J	U	Q	J	K	X	U	X	D	A	N	D	R	V
Y	X	R	Z	N	D	U	L	K	Q	M	U	S	E	R
N	O	S	M	A	I	L	L	I	W	N	J	A	T	E
Y	P	G	H	N	B	P	A	U	B	O	Y	L	W	O
L	A	U	S	H	D	F	R	H	X	B	D	L	L	N
I	T	V	E	I	T	M	A	R	D	W	H	E	H	I
C	M	D	Z	W	N	M	P	Y	V	L	C	T	Q	P
Q	E	S	N	A	M	C	O	U	D	P	A	U	J	A
C	A	X	O	L	J	L	L	T	Z	B	B	P	O	R
N	D	J	R	S	L	M	H	A	L	X	M	A	Y	K
F	U	N	B	H	V	W	E	I	I	R	A	X	D	K
V	J	C	N	Z	P	O	B	O	Z	R	W	Z	V	S

Solution 52

Solution 53

A	M	A	L	L	E	R	A	S	S	A	P	R	T	U
T	E	U	W	U	Y	C	M	S	A	B	S	P	W	K
J	A	R	Y	A	E	V	P	B	E	L	L	I	N	I
W	Z	K	K	W	L	M	S	C	D	Q	R	G	U	O
V	Z	S	R	L	A	T	K	Q	Q	B	M	G	C	W
G	A	V	M	H	L	E	E	G	V	O	O	D	O	K
G	V	S	C	A	N	O	D	R	L	A	O	V	M	A
T	L	S	O	B	T	I	R	C	T	Z	R	Q	B	G
T	E	Z	A	M	P	T	Z	I	D	O	E	E	I	N
D	R	U	L	V	A	S	H	Z	S	F	B	W	L	F
S	E	H	K	B	U	R	A	A	A	F	P	R	H	A
R	L	O	T	R	E	B	L	A	U	S	E	V	M	F
Z	C	T	W	T	S	A	J	E	U	S	A	H	D	H
A	D	V	U	F	L	T	R	N	R	U	T	N	B	W
U	P	Z	P	R	U	H	T	C	A	R	L	O	S	I

Printed in Great Britain
by Amazon

55488517R00066